HF

.5

Performance Appr
Tool for Staff Deve~~lopment~~

D0790747

Robert D. Brown
University of Nebraska

NEW DIRECTIONS FOR STUDENT SERVICES

MARGARET J. BARR, *Editor-in-Chief*
Texas Christian University

M. LEE UPCRAFT, *Associate Editor*
Pennsylvania State University

Number 43, Fall 1988

Paperback sourcebooks in
The Jossey-Bass Higher Education Series

Jossey-Bass Inc., Publishers
San Francisco • London

Robert D. Brown.
Performance Appraisal as a Tool for Staff Development.
New Directions for Student Services, no. 43.
San Francisco: Jossey-Bass, 1988.

New Directions for Student Services
Margaret J. Barr, *Editor-in-Chief;* M. Lee Upcraft, *Associate Editor*

New Directions for Student Services is published quarterly
by Jossey-Bass Inc., Publishers (publication number USPS
449-070). Second-class postage paid at San Francisco, California, and at
additional mailing offices. POSTMASTER: Send address changes
to Jossey-Bass Inc., Publishers, 350 Sansome Street, San Francisco,
California 94104.

Editorial correspondence should be sent to the Editor-in-Chief,
Margaret J. Barr, Sadler Hall, Texas Christian University,
Fort Worth, Texas 76129.

Library of Congress Catalog Card Number LC 85-644751

International Standard Serial Number ISSN 0164-7970

International Standard Book Number ISBN 1-55542-896-7

Cover art by WILLI BAUM

Manufactured in the United States of America. Printed on acid-free paper.

Ordering Information

The paperback sourcebooks listed below are published quarterly and can be ordered either by subscription or single copy.

Subscriptions cost $48.00 per year for institutions, agencies, and libraries. Individuals can subscribe at the special rate of $36.00 per year *if payment is by personal check.* (Note that the full rate of $48.00 applies if payment is by institutional check, even if the subscription is designated for an individual.) Standing orders are accepted.

Single copies are available at $11.95 when payment accompanies order. (California, New Jersey, New York, and Washington, D.C., residents please include appropriate sales tax.) For billed orders, cost per copy is $11.95 plus postage and handling.

Substantial discounts are offered to organizations and individuals wishing to purchase bulk quantities of Jossey-Bass sourcebooks. Please inquire.

Please note that these prices are for the calendar year 1988 and are subject to change without notice. Also, some titles may be out of print and therefore not available for sale.

To ensure correct and prompt delivery, all orders must give either the *name of an individual* or an *official purchase order number.* Please submit your order as follows:

Subscriptions: specify series and year subscription is to begin.
Single Copies: specify sourcebook code (such as, SS1) and first two words of title.

Mail orders for United States and Possessions, Latin America, Canada, Japan, Australia, and New Zealand to:
Jossey-Bass Inc., Publishers
350 Sansome Street
San Francisco, California 94104

Mail orders for all other parts of the world to:
Jossey-Bass Limited
28 Banner Street
London EC1Y 8QE

New Directions for Student Services Series
Margaret J. Barr, *Editor-in-Chief;* M. Lee Upcraft, *Associate Editor*

Contents

Foreword

I remember telling a supervisor once that I needed to improve my teaching skills. For several years after that, I was rated low on those skills by that same supervisor. It was not until I was given a teaching award that I was finally out from under the criticism that I had heaped on myself. Such experiences can lead to an attitude of "whatever you do, do not admit weaknesses to a supervisor." This is unfortunate because such an attitude limits the coaching or mentoring that can take place.

One year, when reading other staff members' end-of-the-year self-evaluations, I was unpleasantly surprised. A sentence that appeared in all the self-assessments with little variation was "This has been the best year of my entire career." The process, I realized, must be dehumanizing if it led each staff member to make this and similar self-aggrandizing statements. Everyone, apparently, shared my own conclusion about not admitting weaknesses and had added to it a new rule of thumb: Say not only good things about yourself, but great things.

Other brief horror stories about performance appraisals are chronicled throughout this sourcebook. Performance appraisal is an activity that goes on whether we think we are doing it or not. Most of it is informal. Much of it is shoddy. Too much of it is harmful and deserves the bad image it often has. This is particularly unfortunate because so much potential is being wasted.

If supervisors could view performance appraisal just as as coaches view working with athletes or as mentors view working with their students, evaluation would help more staff become better professionals. I recognize that not all coaches are patient angels and that not all mentors are altruistic, but if performance appraisal was approached with the same ideal we have for coaching and mentoring, then its bad reputation would soon melt away.

This sourcebook presents the necessary steps in designing, implementing, and using an effective performance appraisal system. Throughout the book, I address comments to "you." In most instances, that "you" is someone in a supervisory relationship. It could be a hall director who supervises student assistants, it could be a director of residence life who supervises the hall directors, or it could be the vice-president for student affairs who supervises all staff. The "you" could be someone in a small college or a large university; the principles are applicable in a variety of settings. The "you" could also be a staff team that is responsible for designing or implementing a performance appraisal system for their student affairs unit.

1

Chapter One discusses the need for a performance appraisal system, presents a definition of performance appraisal, and discusses the ways in which it is a system. Chapter Two addresses the question of whether or not you need a performance appraisal system and outlines the events that must occur when you design such a system. Developing performance appraisal tools and strategies is the focus of Chapter Three. Issues related to who should be involved in the appraisal and what training is necessary are the focus of Chapter Four. Goal-setting activities with staff are an important element of performance appraisal, and these are discussed in Chapter Five. Appraisal interviews are the subject of Chapter Six, and Chapter Seven looks at frequent problems that arise in appraising staff performance. Chapter Eight presents the key concepts and questions you need to have in mind when you evaluate the effectiveness of the system. Finally, Chapter Nine offers a few thoughts and a brief list of helpful sources.

This sourcebook is intended to stimulate and guide student affairs administrators and staff members who are creating a performance appraisal system. The book proposes that performance appraisal must be viewed as a process and a system rather than as an end-of-the-year event or as a rating form. It also suggests that administrators and staff need training in performance appraisal processes and techniques and that both need to be heavily involved in the design and implementation of the system. An effective performance appraisal system involves knowledgeable and skilled administrators who participate creatively in designing and implementing the system, and staff who rate others fairly and objectively and who know how to make the best use of the system for their professional and personal development.

Robert D. Brown

Robert D. Brown is the Carl A. Happold Distinguished Professor of Educational Psychology at the University of Nebraska, Lincoln. He is editor of the Journal of College Student Development *and has written extensively on mentoring programs, student residence life innovations, applied ethics, and program evaluation in higher education.*

Performance appraisal is a system that includes
important processes as well as key events.

The Need for and Purpose of a Performance Appraisal System

Scenario 1: Susan has been vice-president for student affairs for one year and is starting her second year. She has concluded that she has reasonably adequate middle managers who have hard-working staffs, but both groups seem tired, burned out, and committed to maintaining the status quo. Few, if any, seem interested in or have the time to take on new projects.

Scenario 2: A female staff member in the financial aid office was released by the director. She is suing because of alleged discriminatory treatment. She says she was fired without notice, but the director tells you that she never performed adequately. The director indicates, however, that there are no records of performance ratings nor any indication that she was informed of her deficiencies.

Scenario 3: John is residence director at a large university that has thirty residence halls. During his annual review interview at the end of his second year, the director of housing tells him that he ranks in the bottom third of the residence directors; for that reason, he will receive a minimal

R. D. Brown. *Performance Appraisal as a Tool for Staff Development.*
New Directions for Student Services, no. 43. San Francisco: Jossey-Bass, Fall 1988.

salary increase. When John asks what he can do to improve, the director tells him to "work harder."

These are just a few examples of the challenges faced by vice-presidents, directors, and staff members in student affairs. Each represents a performance appraisal problem that might have been prevented or that could be resolved with a good staff evaluation system. This chapter answers three important questions as you begin to explore how you might revamp your own performance appraisal system: (1) Why have a performance appraisal system?, (2) what is performance appraisal?, and (3) what are the essential elements of a performance appraisal system?

Why Have a Performance Appraisal System?

Ask an administrator and a staff member in student affairs what comes to mind when they think of performance appraisal and one of two images are likely to be mentioned: a cumbersome rating form or an uncomfortable annual evaluation interview. The images are negative and narrow.

Every student affairs unit has a performance appraisal system. It may be informal, ineffective, and unsystematic. It may be biased and unorganized. It is likely to be almost invisible and to consist of little more than hearsay, along with a supervisor saying to a staff member at the end of the academic year, "You did a good job. We hope you come back next year." The goal of an appraisal system is not to have highly sophisticated assessment tools or an intricate interview process. The goal is to have an appraisal process that is fair, effective, and one that improves morale and staff performance. Tools, interviews, questionnaires, policies, and procedures are means to an end—the end being that staff members believe their accomplishments are recognized, that they are justly rewarded, and that they have an opportunity to improve professionally. The ultimate goal is that the students' learning environment and the quality of student and staff life on campus are as good as circumstances permit.

A frequent complaint or concern heard from staff members is "I don't what I am being evaluated on" (Brown and others, 1986). It is not unusual for staff members to have received mixed and unclear evaluative messages. What they hear from their supervisors' lips (or what their job description tells them) that they should be doing and how they are rewarded often have no relationship to each other. A residence hall director's job description may be focused primarily on educational and student development goals and activities, but, in an evaluation interview, the director's supervisor comments only on damage reports and discipline issues. A campus activities adviser's job description may discuss the importance of the consultant role, but the dean of students is concerned because several concert and speaker programs have lost money. Both staff members may get no feedback on how their salary increases are related to their job performance.

Most appraisal systems fall short of fulfilling a useful function. There are few examples of appraisals being used for staff development, though organizations in business and industry as well as in higher education espouse staff development as a goal (Berk, 1986). Even where performance appraisal systems exist, there is no ground swell of enthusiasm from administrators or staff about particular models or approaches. Sometimes systems are devised but are never fully implemented, or they are implemented but become systems that run parallel to the real system, which exists in the hallways and behind closed doors. Too often the public system is almost ignored when tough decisions need to be made (Eichel and Bender, 1984). In industry, personnel systems have short lives, do not yield much differentiation in ratings among employees, and are a major source of dissatisfaction to over a fourth of the professional staff (DeVries, Morrison, Shullman, and Gerlach, 1981).

Performance appraisal systems are not intended to focus on problem staff members or to be a way to monitor the day-to-day activities of individual staff. Negative images may accurately reflect the perceptions that many staff members have about their appraisal systems, but that is because most of these systems are poorly designed and implemented. Effective performance appraisal systems focus on the positive: increasing staff morale, recognizing good work, and helping staff members become better professionals. Too often the personnel decisions that come to mind are the ones that involve dealing with a disgruntled staff member or firing a staff member. Thinking about whom to reward, encourage, promote, educate, and coach and how to do these things are also personnel decisions. Helping you make these positive decisions fairly should be the major objective of your appraisal system.

What Is Performance Appraisal?

Staff evaluation has been called *performance appraisal, performance assessment, personnel evaluation,* and *staff appraisal.* Each term has its own connotations. Performance appraisal or evaluation has been defined as the process of identifying, measuring, and developing human performance in organizations (King, 1984). Performance assessment is defined as the process of gathering data by systematic observation for making decisions about an individual (Berk, 1986). *Assessment* implies measurement, and *appraisal* implies placing value or making judgments. The most common term is appraisal. For the purposes of this sourcebook, the term *performance appraisal* will be used because it connotes both assessing and making judgments about worth.

Performance appraisal in this volume, then, is defined as the process of assessing and recording staff performance for the purpose of making judgments about staff that lead to decisions. Its primary purpose is as a tool for staff development. Making judgments about people is a natural process that occurs whether a formal appraisal system exists or not. Administrators make judgments whenever they interact with staff. When a residence hall director handles a crisis in an exceptionally professional manner, the director of housing makes a qualitative judgment and a mental note. If the financial aid director is quite late with an annual report, the vice-chancellor for student affairs makes a judgment about the director's promptness. Evaluations go up the ladder as well as down. When the vice-president for student affairs fails to follow up on a budget promise, the directors and staff members affected will be making judgments. These judgments are a part of normal everyday professional activity. Often they are made on the spot without much deliberation, and often they are stored for use when decisions must be made about the staff member.

The decisions you make will include: providing feedback for professional development, assessing individual and group training needs, determining who is to be promoted, making salary decisions, and selecting new staff. Like the judgments mentioned earlier, these decisions are made regardless of whether or not you have a formal performance appraisal system. You have to decide whether or not a staff member should be funded by the university to attend a professional meeting, what topics and activities should be included in the staff development workshops, who should fill the vacancy in the campus activities office, and what salary increases should be given to the top performers among the directors. Your decisions will be influenced by the appraisal information you have collected.

What Is a Performance Appraisal System?

Performance appraisal should be viewed as a *system*. It is not an event that occurs once a year (as in the traditional end-of-the-year interview), nor is it a form filled out using a five-point scale. A performance appraisal system is a composite of highly interactive processes. These processes involve personnel at all levels (chief executive officers, middle managers, and staff) in differing degrees in determining job expectations, writing job descriptions, selecting relevant appraisal criteria, developing assessment tools and procedures, and collecting, interpreting, and reporting results. An informal system exists just as there are informal evaluative judgments and decisions about staff members, but a more effective system will be carefully planned in its development and deliberate in its implementation. This volume discusses the performance appraisal process as a conscious and deliberate activity.

Good performance appraisal systems have common characteristics and can serve a variety of purposes, but each purpose places an emphasis on acquiring different types of information from the system. If the system is used for staff development purposes, for example, it must provide useful feedback to staff members on directions for professional growth, and it must be viewed as a helpful, nonthreatening process. A system to determine training needs should provide indicators of deficiencies and distinguish environmental constraints from weaknesses in skills. Promotion decisions require indicators that help predict a staff member's performance in a job that involves greater responsibility, as well as indicators of current performance. Using performance appraisals to make salary or other reward decisions demands a process that is accurate, that provides a wide range of performance indicators, and that has credibility among the staff.

Despite these variations, good performance appraisal systems have clearly identifiable common characteristics. These key characteristics are listed below:

1. A student affairs staff and management team coordinates development of the system and monitors its effectiveness.
2. A purpose statement links the appraisal system to the student affairs unit's mission and to its organizational style.
3. A behavioral job description derived from an adequate job analysis serves as the basis for setting goals with each staff member.
4. Job standards provide guidelines for determining adequacy of performance.
5. Top management, middle management, and staff support the system.
6. Appraisal tools and procedures are accurate, reliable, and credible.
7. The appraisal process focuses on behavior rather than on personality traits or attitudes.
8. Training programs exist both for staff involved in conducting appraisals and for those being appraised.
9. Management and staff engage in an ongoing process of setting goals and providing feedback rather than depending only on end-of-the-year review sessions.
10. The interview process focuses on problem solving and staff development.
11. The pervasive orientation is that performance appraisal is an educational and developmental process.

Each of these key elements is discussed in detail in the remaining chapters of this book.

Conclusion

Greater efficiency and productivity are often the benchmarks of good personnel evaluation systems in industry. Greater educational and development outcomes for staff might be more critical benchmarks for performance appraisal systems, particularly in student affairs. If you and your staff view performance appraisal as a process that helps staff learn about themselves and improve their professional skills, then staff morale will be higher, you will enjoy the process more, and efficiency and productivity will naturally follow (Landy, Zedeck, and Cleveland, 1983).

References

Berk, R. A. (ed.). *Performance Assessment.* Baltimore, Md.: Johns Hopkins University Press, 1986.

Brown, R. D., Bond, S., Gerndt, J., Krager, L. A., Krantz, B., Lukin, M., and Prentice, D. "Stress Among Student Affairs Staffs: An Interactional Approach." *NASPA Journal,* 1986, *23* (4), 2-10.

DeVries, D. L., Morrison, A. M., Shullman, S. L., and Gerlach, M. L. *Performance Appraisal on the Line.* New York: Wiley, 1981.

Eichel, E., and Bender, H. E. *Performance Appraisal: A Study of Current Techniques.* New York: American Management Association, 1984.

King, P. *Performance Planning and Appraisal: A How-To Book for Managers.* New York: McGraw-Hill, 1984.

Landy, F., Zedeck, S., and Cleveland, J. *Performance Measurement and Theory.* Hillsdale, N.J.: Erlbaum, 1983.

The design process requires the support of the top student
affairs officers and the involvement of the staff.

Designing a Performance Appraisal System

Scenario: After a spring administrative meeting at which
the president of Vine-Covered University suggested that
each administrative unit examine its performance appraisal
process, Mary D., vice-president for student affairs, decided
to revamp her appraisal system. She wrote to several colleagues around the country and to all her administrative
counterparts whose institutions, like Vine-Covered University, were members of the Football Country Conference. She
requested information about their performance appraisal
process—booklets, forms, and policy statements. She
received fifteen responses out of twenty requests: Five respondents indicated they had a performance appraisal process
consisting primarily of an interview, five responded that
they were working on a process but did not have any written documents or policy statements, and five sent one-page
(a couple used both sides of the page) rating forms.

The forms were remarkably similar. Mary had her
administrative assistant look for the common and unique
items on the five forms and asked him to collapse them
into one master form. She passed out copies of the resulting
two and one-half pages at her next directors' staff meeting,
asking each director to send her comments about what
items to keep or drop. She received two replies. She pruned

R. D. Brown. *Performance Appraisal as a Tool for Staff Development.*
New Directions for Student Services, no. 43. San Francisco: Jossey-Bass, Fall 1988.

the form to two pages, had them printed back to back, and forwarded the form to her unit directors, advising them to use the form to rate all staff. She requested that they forward a copy of the completed rating forms to her office where they would be summarized. That spring she reported to the president that student affairs had installed a systemwide performance appraisal system.

Is this scenario unusual? Probably not. Portraying staff evaluation or performance appraisal as the completion of a rating form is the norm. It is quite likely that, in the beginning, one institution devised a performance appraisal rating form, which has served as a model and has been handed down with only minor revisions as it has changed hands. The original version is still recognizable. This chapter comments on such mistaken views of performance appraisal, describes why performance appraisal needs to be looked at as a system, and enumerates the necessary events in designing a performance appraisal system.

Mistaken Views of Performance Appraisal

The prevailing image of performance appraisal as a form to fill out or a one-shot annual interview suggests that staff and administrators think of appraisal primarily as an event rather than as a process. They see the appraisal occurring at specific times, seldom more than once or twice a year—a goal-setting interview at the beginning of the year and an end-of-the-year annual review. For many middle-level managers, appraisal means completing forms on which they rate staff on a variety of traits. Instructions read, "On a 1–5 scale, rate the staff member on the listed characteristics." What often follows is a list of adjectives such as "dependable," "likable," and "helpful." Often these managers rate the staff member as "outstanding" on every trait because anything less than perfect is viewed as negative. The resulting ratings are essentially useless for the administrator in making decisions about individual staff members.

Performance Appraisal Viewed as a System

Analyses of personnel evaluation systems in numerous managerial settings have revealed that the rating form and the evaluation interview often have no relationship to each other (Conference Board, 1977). Similarly, relationships between what the staff member is really expected to do on the job and what is measured on the evaluation rating form or even what is talked about in the annual review interview are too often purely coincidental. It is easy to understand why most performance appraisal procedures are not highly successful: The efforts lack integration.

If the appraisal process is to result in improved performance and to foster staff development, it must be viewed as a system. It must be an organized, comprehensive, and ongoing process. A system is like a highly interactive organism; when changes occur in one part of the system, they affect all of its other parts. Including items on a performance rating form that are unrelated to the staff members' jobs will eventually diminish the credibility of the form and may also influence what the staff member does in the future. If a counseling center staff member knows, for example, that he is going to be rated on how much he interacts with other student affairs staff, this knowledge could shape his behavior during the year—leading to more contacts with other student affairs agencies. If the director of financial aid knows that she will be rated by other directors but not by her staff, her interactions with her staff may be different than if her staff members' ratings were forwarded directly to the vice-president for student affairs. These interactive effects occur whether or not they are intended. Each element of the appraisal process needs to be intentionally and appropriately linked to the other elements.

Designing a performance appraisal system is not a linear process. Like the appraisal process itself, the design process is highly interactive. It is like a spiral with recurring needs and issues. Because of this, the description of the actions necessary to design an appraisal system and the actions necessary to implement the system are presented as *recurring events* rather than as steps. Figure 1 places the events before you in a circular format. The lines that connect all the points on the circle suggest that each event may reflect backward or forward to another point on the circle. Findings from the job analysis have an impact on writing the job descriptions and establishing job standards, but certain findings may warrant reconsideration of the tie between the mission of the organization and the performance appraisal system or even the composition of a design team. The descriptions that follow discuss each of these recurring events in detail and illustrate their interactive nature.

Deciding to Design a System

Before launching a major design or redesign effort, you must consider whether or not the effort is worth it. Is this something that you or your supervisor read about recently and decided maybe it was time you looked into it? This motivation is fine, but it is probably not sufficient to carry a design team through a lengthy planning process. Several questions need to be considered: Is there an organizational commitment to the design effort? Does this effort have the support of the administration and the staff? What problems or issues prompt the need to redesign the system? How much can be done within specified time limits and within allowable resources? Are you and the staff willing to spend the necessary time on the redesign effort?

Figure 1. Recurring Events in Designing
a Performance Appraisal System

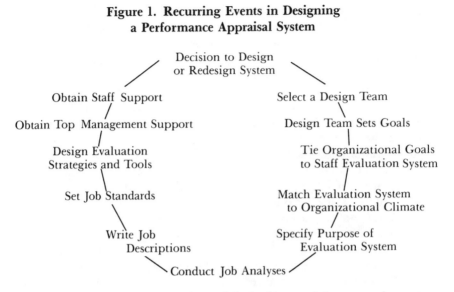

Decision to Design
or Redesign System

Obtain Staff Support

Obtain Top Management Support

Design Evaluation
Strategies and Tools

Set Job Standards

Write Job
Descriptions

Select a Design Team

Design Team Sets Goals

Tie Organizational Goals
to Staff Evaluation System

Match Evaluation System
to Organizational Climate

Specify Purpose of
Evaluation System

Conduct Job Analyses

Going through the motions of designing an elaborate performance appraisal system that is never implemented can have a greater negative impact on staff morale and behavior than trying to live with an inadequate system. You may be the only one who sees the need for a better system, and you may feel strongly enough about it to want to forge ahead. If so, you must be willing to invest the necessary time and energy to convince others of its value and importance. Even the best-designed system that also has the strong support of a major administrator will not succeed unless there is broader support among directors and other middle-management staff.

So one of the first tasks is to consider the need for revising or for initiating a performance appraisal system and to establish rough guidelines as to the time and effort that should be devoted to the task. You may assign the task of exploring the need for a system to a subcommittee of your directors with participation from other members of the staff. This task force might be given a limited charge: Do we need to change our performance appraisal process?

Assigning a Design Team

Even a spiral has a starting point; for a performance appraisal system, the starting point is to have a team or committee assigned to work with you on the development process. Appraisal systems depend for their success on the full cooperation and understanding of managers and staff at all levels, and yet most are designed from the top down. In the scenario that opens this chapter, for example, an administrator solicits rating forms from other administrators, makes a few minor revisions, and then sends it out for all of her staff to use. No one else gets involved in the process.

Four groups of people can serve as the nucleus of a design team: external consultants, internal specialists, middle managers, and other staff. External consultants may include performance appraisal experts from the business and management faculty on campus, private consultants from outside the university, or persons from other university student affairs staffs who have recently undergone a similar design effort. You may especially want to consider involving an external consultant if you are starting completely from scratch. The consultant can be someone who stimulates the staff to consider the relevant issues and who defines the characteristics of a good appraisal system. External assessment experts can provide valuable assistance in making the process psychometrically sound. Management consultants might provide guidance on how to discern administrator and staff concerns.

Employing external experts, however, does not guarantee a perfect appraisal system. External consultants, for example, are unlikely to be familiar with the unique needs of your institution and staff. Their involvement can also be quite expensive. If funds permit, a consultant can train your staff or serve as a resource person at critical moments in the design process.

Internal consultants might be available from within student affairs. Several staff members have had previous experience at another institution or in a business setting; others may have had graduate training in related fields. One staff member might be given released time to do library work and gather resources that will be helpful to the design team. It is particularly valuable to have someone on the team who has experience in developing questionnaires and rating forms and in establishing observation procedures, interview schedules, and job analysis procedures. Using internal consultants has advantages besides that of being less costly. Such consultants are more likely to know the ins and outs of your institution, and they can be available throughout the process to provide critiques and suggestions.

Involvement of staff at all levels increases the possibility that the appraisal process will be relevant and useful. Staff members may not have the technical expertise, but they are in an excellent position to see that the process is realistic, understandable, and accurate. They will be able to tell you if your system is too complicated or cumbersome. They will know what staff behaviors are relevant and what procedures may antagonize other staff members.

Key characteristics of the design team should be knowledge, credibility, and representativeness. The team should have within its ranks sufficient knowledge to be able to ask the right questions of other experts.

Because acceptance of staff and upper management is necessary, the team members should be persons who are trusted by staff and who have access to top-level management. The team should represent major divisions within student affairs or within the unit. A reasonable size is six to ten members (DeVries, Morrison, Shullman, and Gerlach, 1981).

This team can help answer the following questions: What are the essential criteria? What should be asked? Who should be asked? How should the information be used? Are the right questions being asked clearly of the right people?

Because the appraisal system may serve multiple purposes, administrators may want to make the final determination of what goes into the system: They may want or need information in a particular form. But, regardless of how much authority the administrators delegate to the design team, there is no substitute for the involvement of the staff members who will be appraised by the system and who will themselves be using the system. This involvement serves several purposes: It helps remove any mystery from the appraisal process, it provides administrators with ideas for formats and procedures they would not have thought of otherwise, and it increases the sense of ownership in the system for those who will be most affected by it.

Setting Goals

An early task for the design team is to determine the specific goals and boundaries of their task. Are they going to carry through on all phases of the process? Are they going to delegate parts of the design process to other individuals or teams? Perhaps the team might serve as the coordinators while others are involved in conducting job analyses, writing job descriptions, or designing rating scales. The team might form subcommittees to work on the individual tasks. Choosing among these different strategies will depend on the composition of the team, the availability of resources, and the time lines. Participation as a member of a design team can become a staff development activity; members will learn more about their unit, other units, and the entire student affairs office.

Linking the Organizational Mission to the Appraisal System

Your institution and your student affairs units should have well-defined mission statements that can be translated into policy statements, major objectives, and division or unit goals. The more your staff understands the why and what of their jobs as well as the when, where, and how much, the more likely they are to be satisfied and contributing members. Performance appraisal can be the primary link between the organizational mission and what staff members do. If the institutional mission statement (or, in particular, the mission statement of your specific unit) is ambiguous and has never been examined for how it influences expectations about staff behavior and accomplishments, then your performance appraisal system will be mired in a swamp with unforeseen problems rising from the murky darkness. Clear, concise, and specific mission statements should influence budget decisions, allocation of staff time, and what staff do daily. What staff do, in turn, is influenced by what is expected of them and on what basis they are appraised; both are important ingredients in a performance appraisal system.

Conflicts between organizational missions, on the one hand, and individual expectations and behaviors on the other, are quite possible within student affairs. Counseling center staff members may find counseling severely disturbed students more rewarding professionally than participating in career development workshops. Campus activities directors may be caught in their own catch-22 of trying to develop leadership skills and autonomy in campus leaders (which means allowing risk-taking behavior and failure to occur) while they suspect that other campus officials reward them strictly for successful campus events. The vice-president for student affairs may see his or her role as primarily bringing student services needs to the attention of other administrators, whereas the directors and staff see the need for organizational leadership. These and other conflicts can be even further intensified if the organizational mission, individual goals, and the appraisal process are not linked appropriately.

You can picture organizational or unit goals and staff performance as a cascading waterfall with the goals spilling out in a top-down fashion (Raia, 1974). From this perspective, the campus activities director delivers the goals for her unit to her staff who provide input into how the goals are accomplished but accept the goals as givens. The alternative image of a self-replenishing fountain with the goals rising from a spring and then spilling down is more appealing. The fountain analogy suggests that the staff has input into the nature of the goals as well as how they are implemented. This has direct implications for staff performance. Staff are more likely to be satisfied and to perform at a higher level when they have had a part in determining unit goals as well as their personal goals (Latham and Wexley, 1981).

Matching the Appraisal System to the Organizational Climate

Student affairs units across the country have similar goals and organizational units, but different organizational patterns and administrative styles make the organizational climate on each campus unique. Several dimensions of the organizational climate must be considered when designing a performance appraisal system.

If the participatory approach to design and implementation is employed, as suggested throughout this sourcebook, in a context where all other decisions are made in a top-down manner, then staff and administrators will feel awkward, and the resulting system is not likely to be successful. Strong top-down administrative climates would not be compatible with a highly participatory performance appraisal system. A mismatch in the opposite direction can also create problems. If the organizational climate is highly collegial but the performance appraisal system emphasizes the supervisor's role as the ultimate performance rater, this may create confusion and distress when day-to-day relationships are threatened by highly formal evaluation policies.

Different performance appraisal systems may be at the opposite ends of the spectrum in terms of structure and formality. Successful systems usually require planned behavior and concentrated activity; thus, planners of a system need to consider the amount of structure and formality that is compatible with the existing management's style. An administrator who prefers to operate on an impromptu basis from crisis to crisis might wish to delegate aspects of the appraisal system's administration. There is some risk in delegation, however. If important dimensions of the process are relegated to a lower-echelon staff person, the unit's staff may interpret this to mean that the appraisal process is not very important.

Specifying the Purpose

The primary uses of performance appraisal are for promoting staff development and making decisions about salaries and rewards. Whether or not staff development and salary or reward purposes should be combined in the same system is somewhat controversial. It is difficult to separate the two completely, either for the person doing the appraising or for the staff member being appraised. An academic advising staff member, for example, is less likely to admit a weakness to a supervisor if that supervisor is making salary recommendations than if the supervisor is primarily a mentor. This issue will be discussed further as implementation issues are described in Chapters Four through Six. Most experts agree, however, that discussions with staff members about promotion and salary issues should be held separately from mentoring or coaching sessions.

In any case, specifying the purpose or purposes of the appraisal system is an important task during the design phase because, as was mentioned earlier, each purpose has an impact on the kind of information that is collected and on the way in which the appraisal is conducted.

Conducting a Job Analysis

Job analysis is the systematic collection of job-related information for a position, including what is to be done, how it is to be done, and why it is to be done (Beatty, 1982). A thorough job analysis is a prerequisite to a good job description. What is the staff member expected to do on his job? What would not get done if the staff position did not exist? The job analysis process and the resulting job description affect numerous other performance appraisal functions, including selecting criteria, determining training needs, and making job classifications for career ladders.

Conducting a job analysis can be a highly formal, technical process using sophisticated quantitative or qualitative procedures. It can also be relatively informal. The more complex the position is and the higher the level of the position, the more difficult it is to characterize the job in observable and measurable terms. Enumerating the responsibilities of a residence hall assistant is easier than describing the duties of the director of housing, which, in turn, is easier than writing a description of the role and activities of the vice-president for student affairs.

Conducting a job analysis will be an educational experience for staff members and administrators, and the process itself has value independent of the worth of the product, a job description. The thinking and decision making that must be done by the design team during the process provide participants with new insights into their unit's operation and the responsibilities of their colleagues as well as with greater clarity about their own responsibilities.

An initial job analysis can be accomplished by the seat-of-the-pants method (an administrator specifies what she sees as the job tasks), through an armchair approach (experts outline the tasks), or through a watch-them-do-it behavioral analysis (records and observations are used to determine essential tasks). Whatever approach or combination of approaches is used, the job analysis needs to include these three steps:

1. The first step is to break the job down into its major tasks and subtasks. The major tasks of a residence hall director, for example, include training and supervising students assistants, advising the residence hall government, providing educational programs, and maintaining hall discipline. Each major task can then be broken down further into subtasks. How detailed the task analysis needs to be depends on the purpose of the performance appraisal and how detailed you want the appraisal feedback to be. An appraisal intended to provide feedback on how specific performance behaviors can be improved needs to be more detailed than a more global appraisal whose purpose is to provide one indicator to help decide what staff members will be asked back next year.

An excellent organizational framework for a task analysis within student affairs is the list of major roles delineated by Delworth, Hanson, and Associates (1980). These roles include counselor, educator, ecologist, and administrator. Each job task could be assigned to one of these categories. You will find it interesting to note, as the task analysis is completed, how the tasks are distributed across the roles. It may be revealing to find that a position thought to require primarily a counselor or educator role in actuality comprises mostly management activities and responsibilities.

2. After the job is broken down into its component tasks, each task is rated as to its relative importance. Several different groups can provide input with their ratings. You might have current staff provide ratings as well consumers (such as students) and other staff members or experts. The resulting ratings could provide interesting information for a future staff meeting. For example, information on how incumbent staff members' ratings on what is important compare to the ratings of experts and other staff would probably stimulate a healthy discussion.

3. A final step is the collection of critical incidents that typify poor, adequate, and exceptional performance (Fivars, 1975; Flanagan, 1954). Examples of poor performance by a campus activities staff member include being continually late for a student organization's planning meeting or dominating a meeting by overruling the organization's student officer with statement like "I don't think that is a good idea, it never worked before." Making occasional and appropriate process comments during a meeting, such as "It might be helpful to brainstorm possible solutions to this problem" or "If I were to summarize what I have heard thus far at this meeting, it would go something like this . . . ," might be illustrations of adequate performance. Exceptional performance might include creating role-playing exercises, designed to help prevent role conflicts for an organization's workshop for faculty advisers and student leaders.

Supervisors, peers, subordinate staff, and students can be asked to provide examples of staff behavior that fit into the different qualitative categories. Current staff members can also be asked for examples, though incumbents are not as objective in providing examples of ineffective behavior as they are in providing examples of effective behavior (Vroom and Maier, 1961). The process of generating, comparing, and categorizing the illustrative incidents could be provocative as well as educational for current staff within an administrative unit. Incongruencies between what the staff do on the job and what they and others expect them to be doing can lead to soul searching and possible changes in behavior in the future. Thinking about what behaviors reflect stellar job performance can also lead to reconsidering career goals and aspirations, as staff will undoubtedly compare their personal performance with the examples of exceptional performance that surface during the job analysis.

Decisions about who should be involved in conducting the job analysis and about the depth of the analysis should be based on your needs and resources. You may wish to use one process for paraprofessional positions, another process for staff positions, and still another for director positions. You may wish to delegate determination of the process to the persons reporting directly to you and let them decide how they want to proceed with their staff. Everyone involved in planning and implementing a performance appraisal system will find that being part of the design team and assisting in carrying out a job analysis are time-consuming tasks. Top management in student affairs must be committed to supporting these efforts and to following through on recommendations. You may do long-term damage to staff morale and risk staff being less enthusiastic about future committee work if tasks as important and demanding as these are left to wither on an administrative vine.

Writing a Job Description

Most job descriptions are insufficient; they are too vague and not descriptive. Many job descriptions include personal characteristics (such as whether the staff member or director is organized or dependable) rather than job-related behaviors (such as whether the staff member works with roommate complaints or serves as an adviser to a judiciary board). A good job description is reliable, valid, understandable, and specific enough so that is provides direction for staff behavior. The job description can take several forms. It can focus on what the staff member does (for example, "provides students with directions for organizing a residence hall government") or on what outcomes are expected (for example, "residence hall students view the hall as being a good place to study"). A combination of these two is best. Many student affairs staff members possess a caring, attentive, and personal approach to their job, but it is still important that they get the job done. Staff need to know that a caring, personal approach is compatible with meeting deadlines, being on time for meetings, and carrying their share of the routine administrative tasks. Focusing on process to the exclusion of producing a product or accomplishing a goal can lead to individuals and administrative units working solely on day-to-day maintenance activities and never developing new or improving current programs.

The job description should use action words like "plans" or "supervises" rather than "demonstrates initiative" or "is likable." As much as possible, the description should provide guidelines for staff so they know the specific behaviors they are expected to perform. The responsibilities should be listed in order of importance and, if possible, weighted as to importance. The same process used in the job analysis can be used to obtain priorities and weightings. Experts, supervisors, students, coworkers, and staff members can rank the responsibilities or assign weights. (See Henderson, 1980, for a description of a ranking and weighting process.)

Listing the traits of people in student affairs positions is probably so ingrained that it will be difficult to eliminate. It is not unusual to see a job description that says the person must be patient, understanding, dependable, and get along with people well. If you believe you must include these traits in your job descriptions, ask yourself how you will assess them. How will you know a staff member is patient? Does "getting along well with students" mean having no discipline problems, or does it mean spending time listening to student concerns? Make sure you are not too casual and assume that you know a patient person when you see one. It is not possible to measure precisely all the characteristics or behaviors relevant to positions in student services, but it is possible to improve on current efforts. Part of doing better involves writing job descriptions that include descriptions of job behavior rather than personal traits.

You may question the need for a detailed job description for professional positions. After all, isn't a professional supposed to know what to do and when to do it? Shouldn't a professional have latitude to make judgments along the way? Shouldn't there be greater flexibility for the professional staff member? This is all true—within limits. But it is also true that uncertainty about expectations and standards is one of the major sources of stress for professional staff members (Brown and others, 1986). Expectations that are not spelled out clearly can lead to problems for staff and administrators. It is stressful for staff to try to fulfill all job expectations without a sense of priorities. It is difficult for administrators to make decisions about a staff member who has performed in an outstanding manner on one task that met the needs of a select group of students but who was expected to provide services for many other students.

Clear and concise job descriptions with responsibilities ranked and weighted can be used by the administrator as a planning tool as well as an appraisal tool. Precise numerical weighting may not be necessary when working with professional staff, but rough guidelines are helpful (for example, "I think having several hall programs on alcohol abuse is twice as important as having the hall involved in the maximum number of intramural leagues"). If good discipline and low damage reports are important to you, as the supervisor, then the hall director should be aware of this. If, as counseling center director, you place more value on planning and conducting outreach programs than on the number of long-term clients a counselor has, this should be known to staff members. You may not wish to have these priorities assigned specific percentages of time or weighting factors, but these priorities should at least be made clear in your planning sessions with group and individual staff members.

Conducting a thorough job analysis and having comprehensive and specific job descriptions are not going to solve all performance appraisal problems, but they are critical links in the system. How well your job description accurately reflects what is done and what is expected to be done will directly affect the reliability and validity of your appraisals.

Setting Standards

A standard is a quality index that describes performances as acceptable or exceptional with possible gradations in between. Should the standard be what is minimally acceptable, or should it be higher? Several good reasons exist for having standards describe acceptable behavior. Standards that typify acceptable behavior rather than exceptional behavior have the potential, if appropriately used, to increase staff morale and provide more flexibility in an appraisal system. If a staff member does not meet the standards for acceptable performance, this clearly points out the need for remedial action. Awareness of deficiencies can provide direction for staff development needs, special training or supervision, or possible reassignment. Persons reaching the acceptable performance level should have a sense of accomplishment; with the standard set at the acceptable level, more people will attain this goal, as contrasted to the dissatisfaction and discomfort possible if many do not reach standards that are set above the acceptable level. When the standard describes what is acceptable, staff have the opportunity to surpass the standard, be recognized for their performance, and be especially satisfied with their accomplishments.

Like the job description, standards should focus on job behavior and job expectations rather than on personal characteristics, and they should be communicated to and agreed on by the staff. Good standards also must: (1) be achievable, (2) be understandable, (3) be specific and as measurable as possible, (4) be written, (5) be flexible, (6) specify a schedule and time limits, and (7) indicate the quality and quantity of effort expected (Kirkpatrick, 1982). Standards for a campus activities adviser might include how many organizations he advises, behavioral indices of what constitutes good advising (such as the number of advising sessions or involvement of student leaders in planning), characteristics of reports, confidence that student leaders have in his advice, and how well he conducts meetings and uses available resources.

Standards should focus on what the staff member can control. Holding staff members responsible for the number of racial incidents in a residence hall, for example, is not as appropriate as expecting them to have appropriate programs, discussions, and dialogues in the halls that deal with racial issues and as appraising how they respond to the incidents. The staff member can be held accountable for providing an environment and a leadership style that are conducive to student development but not held accountable for every unfortunate incident. This issue will be discussed again in Chapter Five.

Achievement standards should be related to job needs and accomplishments and should not consist of comparisons with the performance of other staff members. Do not set standards that imply comparisons between units or with units on other campuses. It is not helpful for performance appraisal purposes to know that the financial aid office sees more students than the counseling center or that the campus activities office spends more time with students from the Greek system than do the Greek student advisers. What is critical is what were the expectations for each of these staffs and whether or not these were met. Good standards should help staff members plan their work better—by helping them set their priorities—and should provide the administrator and the individual staff member with clear performance guidelines.

Obtaining Top-Level Support

Whatever form the appraisal system takes and whatever administrative unit uses it, the system must have the support of top management. Lack of support by chief executive officers is one of the most frequently cited reasons for failure of performance appraisal systems (DeVries, Morrison, Shullman, and Gerlach, 1981). Even if the administrative location of the system is closer to the directors' level than to that of the chief student affairs officer, there are several ways in which the chief student affairs officer can provide support. Only the chief student affairs officer, for example, can ensure that effective appraisal practices are, in turn, a significant criterion in the appraisal of middle managers (directors or department and agency heads). In addition, how the chief student affairs officer evaluates his or her immediate line staff—the directors—can be a model for the directors themselves. How can you expect directors to spend time and energy on performance appraisal if their own performance is evaluated in a cavalier or impromptu fashion?

Obtaining Staff Support

Probably more than any other design task, this is clearly not an event but an ongoing process. Staff involvement has been highlighted as essential through each phase of the design process. But it does not end with completion of the design; it must be carried forward into the implementation phase. Ultimately, staff support will be contingent on how well the system is implemented. As noted in the remaining chapters, there are ample opportunities to botch the process. If you use the summary checklist that follows, you will have reduced the probability of botching the process up to this point.

Conclusion

One important design task listed in Figure 1—appraisal tools and strategies—has been omitted from this chapter. The discussion of this process warrants an in-depth examination, which is presented in Chapter Three. You may find the following checklist helpful for determining whether or not you are accomplishing all the necessary tasks in designing your appraisal system.

1. Is the chief student affairs officer committed to performance appraisal?
2. Are staff involved in determining the appraisal criteria and standards?
3. Are the organizational goals of student affairs and subunits integrated into the appraisal plan?
4. Are staff involved in planning the implementation of the appraisal process?
5. Is the appraisal process congruent with the organizational climate and the management style of administrators?
6. Have adequate job descriptions based on job analyses been written?
7. Have weights or priorities been assigned to job expectations?
8. Is available expertise being employed for consultation?
9. Is the purpose of the performance appraisal system clearly articulated and congruent with the staff and management needs and expectations?
10. Has a process been worked out to monitor and evaluate the system (see Chapter Eight)?

References

Beatty, R. W. "Job Analysis and Performance Appraisal." In L. S. Baird, R. W. Beatty, and C. E. Schneier (eds.), *The Performance Appraisal Handbook*. Amherst, Mass.: Human Resource Development Press, 1982.

Brown, R. D., Bond, S., Gerndt, J., Krager, L. A., Krantz, B., Lukin, M., and Prentice, D. "Stress Among Student Affairs Staff: An Interactional Approach." *NASPA Journal*, 1986, *23* (4), 2-10.

Conference Board. *Appraising Managerial Performance: Current Practices and Future Directions*. New York: Conference Board, 1977.

Delworth, U., Hanson, G. R., and Associates (eds.). *Student Services: A Handbook for the Profession*. San Francisco: Jossey-Bass, 1980.

DeVries, D. L., Morrison, A. M., Shullman, S. L., and Gerlach, M. L. *Performance Appraisal on the Line*. New York: Wiley, 1981.

Fivars, G. "The Critical Incident Technique: A Bibliography." *JSAS Catalog of Selected Documents in Psychology*, 1975, *5*, 210-225.

Flanagan, J. C. "The Critical Incident Technique." *Psychological Bulletin*, 1954, *51*, 327-358.

Henderson, R. *Performance Appraisal: Theory to Practice*. Reston, Va.: Reston Publishing, 1980.

Kirkpatrick, D. L. *How to Improve Performance Through Appraisal and Coaching*. New York: AMACOM, 1982.

Latham, G. P., and Wexley, K. E. *Increasing Productivity Through Performance Appraisal*. Reading, Mass.: Addison-Wesley, 1981.

Raia, A. P. *Management by Objectives.* Glenview, Ill.: Scott, Foresman, 1974.

Vroom, V. H., and Maier, N.R.F. "Industrial Social Psychology." *Annual Review of Psychology,* 1961, *12,* 413–446.

Behavioral indicators of performance should form the basis for the selection and development of appraisal tools.

Developing Appraisal Tools and Strategies

Scenario: Jonathon Countemup, vice-president of student affairs at a small college, sends all of his staff a rating form in March along with a list of all staff members in student affairs. He asks them to rate all the other staff members on the rating forms, which list traits such as patience, cooperativeness, model for students, and attention to detail. Several weeks later, he compiles all the forms and computes a mean score for each item and an overall score for each staff member. On the basis of each staff member's overall score, he ranks his staff members from one to twenty. Using these ranks he gives 10 percent raises to the top five staff members, 7 percent raises to the next five, 5 percent to the following five, and 2 percent to the bottom five staff members. He prides himself on how objective and fair this approach is.

Jonathon's approach, on the surface, may seem better than no formal process at all, but this may not necessarily be true. The assessment process

R. D. Brown . *Performance Appraisal as a Tool for Staff Development.*
New Directions for Student Services, no. 43. San Francisco: Jossey-Bass, Fall 1988.

and tools need to match the purpose of the appraisal. Carpenters use a saw to cut lumber and a hammer to pound a nail; administrators evaluating their staff need to use the right assessment process and tools. Using the wrong tool can easily make the process inefficient and painful and will undoubtedly result in shoddy appraisals. The interactive nature of different components of a performance appraisal system is particularly apparent when considering the appraisal tools. Choice of the tool affects staff morale, the appraisal climate, and affects and is affected by the reward system. This chapter describes the advantages and disadvantages of three appraisal strategies: ranking, behavioral rating, and goalsetting.

Ranking

Definition. Before discussing the uses of a ranking system, we must distinguish between ranking and rating. Ranking and rating are two frequently used appraisal strategies, and unfortunately the terms are often confused and misused. Ranking staff members means placing them in order from one to whatever the bottom rank would be for the last person. For ten staff members, each person would be given a rank from one to ten. A performance ranking indicates relative performance in comparison to others being ranked. Depending on the ranking system used, two or more people may have the same rank (implying that they are not distinguishable from each other). But ties are rare, so most ranking systems result in each person having a distinct rank.

Rating, on the other hand, means comparing each staff member's performance to a standard, usually on specific performance dimensions. Respondents circle a number that indicates their perceptions of how well the staff member performed or how well he or she matches up with a particular standard. A typical rating form might ask a supervisor to rate on a 1-to-5 scale on how well each housing director provided leadership for his or her staff. It is conceivable that all housing directors could be given the highest possible rating.

The information obtained from ratings can be used to rank the staff. This is what Jonathon did in the opening scenario. He used compilations of summated ratings across dimensions to rank the staff. It is not possible to derive ratings, however, from ranks. A rating score tells you how high or low a staff member was rated overall or on a particular dimension. (For example, Susan's average rating on supervising paraprofessionals was 4.25 on a five-point scale; her overall average rating was 4.33 on a five-point scale.) A ranking tells you a staff member's relative position compared to others. (For example, Susan was ranked ninth out of twenty staff members.)

Ranking as an Appraisal Tool. Creating lists may be a peculiarly American phenomenon. If it is not unique to this country, it is at least an extremely popular activity. It is nearly impossible to read a magazine without finding a top ten list. It may be a list of the top ten musical records, baseball players, millionaires, fashionably dressed men and women, or cars sold. No matter what the item, apricots or zucchini, or what the characteristic, adroitness or zest, you can find a top ten list. So it is not surprising that you often find yourself in the position of ranking your staff. The important questions are whether or not a ranking system is appropriate at all and whether or not it is handled appropriately.

If you wish to compare staff performances, then ranking is one method. You may decide on salary increases based on staff members' rank, or you may determine who among several candidates should be promoted. Ranking provides minimal information for staff development purposes, however, and can be misused even when applied for appropriate purposes. It is one of the simplest, cheapest, and most used techniques, however, so awareness of the different ranking methods and their strengths and weaknesses is necessary.

Straight Ranking. Three ranking systems are prevalent: straight ranking, forced-distribution ranking, and paired-comparison ranking. Let us look at the simplest system first, the straight ranking system, listing persons from the best to the poorest. At first, it may seem simple enough to rank the staff. Who is number one? Who is at the bottom? These seem like easy questions. But a little more thought prompts other questions that need answering. For example, do you rank the staff on a global basis—who is best overall—or do you rank the staff on key characteristics and behaviors? What if one staff member ranks high in supervising his own staff but low in cooperating with other directors? Should these and similar rankings be averaged or weighted?

In a ranking system, one-half of the staff must be in the lower half, and, of course, someone will be at the bottom. Research suggests that all staff consider their own performance to be average or above average (Henderson, 1980). This means that if the rankings are revealed to individual staff members, even in private interviews where they are told only their personal ranking, half of the staff are going to be told they are in the bottom half. This is not good news to the bottom half. It will not help morale and certainly does not provide guidance about how to change or improve.

Two weaknesses must be noted if rankings are going to be used for determining salary raises. First, it is not possible to compare persons fairly across groups. An individual may be the lowest-ranked staff member in a high-performing unit, but, compared to the performance of staff in another unit, he or she might be average or above. Your financial aid staff, for example, could be the best in the country, but your academic advising unit is extremely weak. The performance of the lowest-ranked staff member among the financial aid staff could be quite adequate, though her rank within her unit is low. If you compare the expectations for her position with her performance, however, she may be performing in a manner comparable to an average or above average performance for the advising staff. If salary increases or other rewards are determined by rank within a unit, then the low-ranked financial aid staff member is being punished for being a member of a high-quality staff. If she had been in another unit and performing at the same level, she might have been given significantly greater recognition.

Second, rankings do not reveal the magnitude of the differences between staff members. Is the staff member ranked as third an equal distance from the second and fourth individuals? Is the distance between second and fourth the same distance as between eighth and tenth? Ranking alone provides no index of these relative differences. The staff members ranked first and second could be quite close; you may find it extremely difficult to choose between them. On the other hand, the distance between second and third may be quite clear, and you have no difficulty making that distinction. Among your top three staff members in campus activities, for example, John and Mary are top-notch performers. They work closely together, they were hired at the same time, and they are equally sought out by other staff and students for advice. Jim is the third best staff member on your criteria. He has been on the staff several more years than John and Mary and, though he does a creditable and consistently good job, there is no comparison between him and John and Mary. Yet, if someone asks you for your top three or four staff members, Jim will be in the same cluster as John and Mary. Is this fair, if, as a result, John, Jim, and Mary are given the same salary increases?

Forced-Distribution Rankings. The failure to provide an index of the magnitude of the differences between persons is particularly a problem if a forced-distribution ranking system is used. This system requires the appraiser to list the staff members with a predetermined percentage of them in categories such as above average, average, and below average. The same issues arise as for the straight ranking system. What if the bottom group is performing at an acceptable level? What if the average group is relatively above average compared to staff in another group?

A forced-distribution ranking system can present legal problems as well as interpretation problems. Use of a bell curve for rankings (a designated percentage of lows and highs) is expressly forbidden in federal regulations (Equal Employment Opportunity Commission, 1979; Latham and Wexley, 1981). Job performance must be evaluated on how it compares to job standards. The key question is how well the staff member is getting the job done, not how the staff member's performance compares to others.

Paired-Comparison Ranking. Less frequently used is the paired-comparison method of ranking. In this method, staff members are compared to each and every person in the same group. Names can be put on cards, for example, and the first step is to pick one card, compare the staff member on this card to the staff member listed on another card, keep the better of the two, and then compare the better staff member to those listed on each of the other cards, continually keeping the better one until only one card is left—the best performer. The process then begins again with the rest of the cards to determine who is second best and so on.

This process is time consuming, and it is difficult to compare more than five persons at a time. The possible paired-comparison combinations is N $(N-1)/2$, where N equals the number of persons. Thus, comparing five persons necessitates ten comparisons, whereas comparing fifteen persons necessitates 105 comparisons.

Weighted Ranking. A modification of an overall ranking system is to rank staff on each of several job performance dimensions and then to use the sum of the individual ranks to determine an overall rank. If this is done, it is important to decide what weight should be given to each dimension. Is performance on developing interagency programs as important as creating a good in-house staff development program? Jonathon, in the opening scenario, summed the ratings to arrive at an overall rank, thus giving equal weight to all of the individual performance dimensions. Making these determinations is not a unique prerequisite for rankings, but it is a necessary consideration if a summated ranking system is going to be used. If relatively few dimensions (between five and ten) are used, a weighting process is not too cumbersome.

There are undoubtedly times when an administrator wants to know who her best staff member is or who her best three staff members are, and so there are times when ranking is necessary and helpful. It is essential, however, to be aware of such a system's weaknesses and potential misuses. Be particularly aware that rankings do not reflect magnitude of differences, and summated rankings across dimensions may inappropriately give greater weight to some performance dimensions than to others.

Behaviorally Anchored Rating Scales (BARS)

Rating scales use words or phrases to identify the degree to which a behavior or characteristic is present. A behavior such as being on time is listed, and raters are asked to indicate on a 1-to-5 scale (where 1 equals "Never" and 5 equals "Always") how frequently the individual exhibits that behavior. In the past, many rating scales have focused on personality traits, and many still do. Trait scales ask raters to indicate how industrious, energetic, cooperative, or conscientious a staff member is. Trait scales are extremely vulnerable to rating errors, which will be discussed

Figure 1. Example of a Behaviorally Anchored Scale

Job Dimension: Planning and Implementing Staff Training Programs

7 ☐   Excellent   Develops a comprehensive plan, includes supportive written materials, and provides time lines and budget information. Implementation goes smoothly. Uses staff and colleague feedback to redesign future programs.

6 ☐   Very Good   Develops detailed plan with time lines and budgets. Has occasional minor implementation problems but makes adjustments with ease.

5 ☐   Good   Has a general plan and fills in details each week. Seldom fails to meet deadlines and budget projections are usually accurate.

4 ☐   Average   Has a plan and revises time lines as the programs near implementation which occasionally causes some delays.

3 ☐   Below Average   Plans are poor: No realistic time lines are provided and budget projections are inaccurate.

2 ☐   Very Poor   Has no work plan and does little or no planning.

1 ☐   Unacceptable   Seldom completes a full-scaled training program because of lack of planning. Does not seek direction or assistance on how to improve.

in Chapter Four. Trait-related rating scales have not fared well in the courts because of the lack of direct ties to job-related performance (DeVries, Morrison, Shullman, and Gerlach, 1981). Though trait-scale ratings may correlate significantly with other indicators of performance, few assessment experts would come to their defense as a substitute for direct performance measures.

The weaknesses of trait scales have bolstered the movement to develop more behaviorally anchored rating scales (BARS) (Kafry, Jacobs, and Zedeck, 1980). BARS ask respondents to rate descriptions of behaviors rather than traits. Consistent with job analysis and job descriptions that focus on behaviors, behaviorally based scales ask raters to compare the person's performance with descriptions of job-related behavior. Instead of the ubiquitous Likert-like scales with "strongly agree" to "strongly disagree" and "always" to "never" as verbal anchors, behavioral scales provide descriptors reflecting behavior, such as "organizes staff development programs" or "has no written plans or schedule for training staff." Figure 1 provides a sample of a behaviorally anchored scale.

Developing a Behaviorally Anchored Scale. The process of developing a behaviorally based rating scale is similar to that of developing a good job description by completing a thorough job analysis. A four-step process follows:

1. Gather critical incidents. What are examples of exceptional, good, average, and poor performance? Collect incidents by having staff members and others provide examples of effective and ineffective job behaviors. Incidents can be gathered as part of a brainstorming activity during a staff meeting, by having selected staff maintain a daily log, or by having middle-management staff shadow selected staff and record critical incidents.

2. Categorize incidents into performance dimensions. In a residence hall setting, for example, behaviors might be classified as staff supervision, residential education programming, or maintenance. The classification process can be done by the same people who provided the critical incidents.

If good job descriptions are available that already have job behaviors classified into categories, these categories can be used as the starting point. The category labels may suggest job behaviors that characterize exceptional to poor performance. A team working on campus activities rating scales, for instance, might think of examples of exceptional or poor job performance for such responsibilities as consulting with organizations on budgets, designing leadership workshops for organization officers, and assisting organizations in developing membership campaigns.

One technique is to give the team members lists of categories and a separate list of job behaviors (perhaps on three-by-five cards) and ask them to place the job behaviors into the appropriate categories. Job behaviors for which there is not 80 percent agreement (say four out of five staff members) that they belong in the same category should be revised or eliminated.

3. Do a reliability check. Double-check the categories by having another group go through the same process. Will another group classify the job behaviors into the same categories and into the same level of performance (good, average, poor)? The team could be divided in half with one half working on developing behavioral descriptions and putting them into categories for one job and the other half doing the same for another job. Then they could trade jobs, with each group seeing if they agree with the other group's categorization. Ideally, this double-checking process should involve the checkers trying to place the job behaviors into categories without knowing the placements made by the first group.

Studies of job performance dimensions or categories for professional positions usually yield similar broad categories (Henderson, 1980). These include: (1) planning, organizing, and setting priorities; (2) technical knowledge and ability to apply knowledge; (3) proficiency in supervising staff; (4) responsiveness to supervision; (5) proficiency in handling administrative detail; and (6) personal commitment. These categories can be used as the framework for categorizing the critical incidents derived from the job behavior descriptions or as a check to decide whether or not the critical incidents are comprehensive.

4. Assign numerical weights. Another group or a combination of persons used in the earlier steps rates each job behavior on a five- or seven-point scale with the high point representing excellent or outstanding job performance and the low score representing poor or inadequate performance. Job behaviors with high interjudge agreement are retained. One measure of agreement is having a standard deviation (that is, an average distance from the mean rating) of less than 1.5 (Latham and Wexley, 1981).

Seldom during the developmental phase of a behaviorally anchored scale will you have a full complement of examples to match numerical ratings from 1 to 5 or 7. You might have examples only of superior and inferior performance or only of average or acceptable behavior. Then you must fill out the scale with job behaviors that represent the missing points. Developing descriptions of extremely good or extremely poor performance is usually easier than arriving at precise descriptors of behavior between these extremes. It is best to have at least five levels; to have seven levels is very good, but it is often difficult to arrive at precise verbal descriptions for all seven. A rating with more than seven levels of behavior can lead to more precision but is even more difficult to develop and often makes the rating task itself more difficult.

How do you know that a descriptor is assigned to the right level? This is difficult to assess with precision. One crude check is to put the job behaviors on cards and ask local experts and staff members to rank them from best to worst. If four out of five give the behaviors the same ranking, you can feel reasonably comfortable about the item.

Cruder versions of BARS are used when it is too difficult or time consuming to develop behavioral anchors for each point. Using behavioral anchors for the most negative or unsatisfactory behavior and the most positive or extremely acceptable behavior is an alternative. Raters are asked to develop their own continuum and to rate the staff member's performance accordingly. Figure 2 provides two examples in which the raters provide their own meanings for 2, 3, and 4; thus, these scores may have different meanings to different raters. It is possible that your 3 may be more like my 4, so there is room for error.

Figure 2. Verbal Anchors at Extreme Points

Circle the number that comes closest to describing the person's behavior

1. Delegation of assignments

Does not delegate	1	2	3	4	5	Delegates tasks appropriately

2. Responsiveness to supervision

Makes defensive comments	1	2	3	4	5	Suggests specific ways behavior will be changed

Another variation is to provide only a midpoint descriptor and ask the raters to provide their own examples of the staff member's performance that fall above or below this midpoint. This open-ended format would be difficult to assess objectively, but, for a relatively small staff, it could be quite informative and could be used as an initial step in formulating a more refined behaviorally anchored scale. In fact, this procedure could be adapted for the first-round use of a BARS. Raters could be asked to use either the given behavioral anchors or to provide their own.

Developing your own behaviorally anchored scales is more complex and costly than adapting somebody else's form and deciding whether to use a "strongly agree" to "strongly disagree" or "always" to "never" format. But the resulting scales are based on relevant performance measures, and the information they provide can be used for feedback purposes as well as for salary and promotion determinations. Having staff members participate in the developmental process helps ensure that a representative sample of critical job behaviors are included and that these behaviors are presented in a form that is clear and understandable. It is not necessary that all staff participate in all phases of the scale's development.

Behavioral Observation and Behavioral Expectation Scales. Two variations of the BARS have evolved: the behavioral observation scale (BOS) and the behavioral expectation scale (BES). The BOS focuses on behavior actually observed by the rater. Raters respond to questions asking them to rate the student services staff member on the basis of behaviors they have observed during a specified period of time, usually the past academic or calendar year. Another variation is to ask the rater, usually the direct supervisor, to observe the staff member's current performance and to rate expected performance or job behavior not directly observed. In this variation, the scale usually includes a five-point frequency rating, from "almost never" to "almost always," for each of the behaviors. Figure 3 illustrates a behavioral observation scale.

When using descriptions that indicate frequency such as "sometimes" and "most of the time," provide a definition of what these words mean. Most raters will be reasonably consistent in their use of "never" and "always," but, when they are given only a series of numbers in between or vague descriptions like "sometimes," consistency breaks down. One rater may consider "sometimes" to mean once a week, another once a month, and still another twice a week. This may mean you have to provide different descriptors for different items, and this is fine; there is nothing magical about using the identical descriptors for every item, nor is efficiency greatly improved. It is better to have accurate descriptors that provide useful information than to have a rating form that appears neat, with uniform descriptors for every item.

Figure 4 provides two examples of providing descriptors that allow

Figure 3. Example of a Behavioral Observation Scale

Job Dimension: Facilitating Change Within an Organization

1. Describes the details of the change to staff.

   Almost Never   1   2   3   4   5   Almost Always

2. Explains to staff why change might be helpful.

   Almost Never   1   2   3   4   5   Almost Always

3. Asks staff for reactions to the idea of change.

   Almost Never   1   2   3   4   5   Almost Always

4. Responds to staff suggestions by revising plans.

   Almost Never   1   2   3   4   5   Almost Always

5. Encourages staff to engage in mutual problem solving on implementing change.

   Almost Never   1   2   3   4   5   Almost Always

more precision than the ubiquitous "strongly agree"-"strongly disagree" format. Rating forms using terms like "average" and "superior" or "satisfactory" and "unsatisfactory" are prevalent. These forms can be improved dramatically if these terms are defined, so the chance of each respondent reading the same meaning into the descriptors is increased. Figure 5 provides sample definitions of descriptors. These are not intended to be used exactly as they appear; they should be modified for your particular use. Most important, you should provide behavioral examples of performance that are "consistent" or "beyond expectations" and so on.

     Behavioral expectation scales (BES) are used for situations when direct observation of the behavior is not always possible. The distinction is an important one. On a behavioral observation scale, raters check behavior they know to have occurred. On a BES scale, they check behavior they would expect to occur. For most staff positions in student services, rating expected behavior is more feasible because it is unlikely that

Figure 4. Precise Verbal Descriptors

The resident assistant visits with high-risk students:

More than once a week	Once a week	Every other week	Once a month	Several times a semester	Once a semester

The resident assistant provides helpful suggestions during staff meetings:

Almost Never (0%-9%)	Infrequently (10%-19%)	Sometimes (20%-39%)	Regularly (40%-69%)	Often (70%-84%)	Almost Always (85%-100%)

Figure 5. Sample Definitions of Descriptive Rating Terms

Exceptional	Performance is clearly outstanding; meets or exceeds highest standards; rare person
Top Performer	Performance is nearly exceptional; person is outstanding but not rare.
Above Average or Highly Effective	Performance consistently meets and at times exceeds expectations
Average or Satisfactory	Overall performance generally meets the basic expectations of the job.
Slightly Below Average	Performance occasionally slips below expectations.
Below Average or Unsatisfactory	Performance is below what should be expected after a reasonable period of time on the job.
Inadequate	Performance is clearly unsatisfactory and fails to meet minimum requirements.
Not Observable or Relevant	Rater does not have sufficient knowledge to rate, or the behavior described is not relevant.

raters will be able to make direct observations. The behavioral anchors, in this case, would be general illustrations of behavior rather than precise examples. Raters are asked to look at the anchor (for example, "student assistant performs job when residence hall director is not present") as an illustration and base their rating on what they would expect to occur.

If the major purpose of the rating scale is to sort out the good performers from the inadequate performers, scale items on which almost everyone is rated high or low can be eliminated because the tabulations will not distinguish between good and poor performers. If the intent is to provide feedback information, however, these same items can be useful in providing praise and encouragement for tasks well done and in indicating staff development needs for tasks rated consistently low.

When you use the information obtained from either BOS or BES scales to make decisions about individual staff members, start with the global categories rather than specific items within them. Are all total scores for each category reasonably consistent, or are there significant variations? Look to see if Mary's ratings for the total category of management responsibilities, for example, are higher or lower than her ratings for the category labeled supervising staff. If one category stands out as dramatically higher than the rest, this provides you with a basis for praise and encouragement. If one category stands out as dramatically lower than the rest, this provides the basis for further discussion. Check to see if the items within this category are consistently low or if there is some variation. This provides you with diagnostic clues for further action.

Behaviorally anchored rating scales are easier to defend legally than are other rating scales (DeVries, Morrison, Shullman, and Gerlach, 1981). These scales also hold more potential for guiding individual staff development than do trait-related scales. They are not completely free, however, from possible rating errors, which will be discussed in Chapter Four. Because you can list only a limited number of specific behaviors in the scales, raters will sometimes have difficulty matching behavior they have observed with the behavior described on the forms. This will be particularly true in the initial design stages. You can always add additional descriptors to the categories, but you should also instruct raters to keep in mind that the descriptors are illustrations and not intended to be precise.

Goal-Attainment Scales

Chapter Five looks at goal setting as a management tool and at its relationship to performance appraisal. Management by objectives (MBO) remains a viable strategy for student affairs administrators. Job responsibilities and task expectations in student affairs vary widely from position to position so that one set of criteria and uniform appraisal forms may not be specific enough to provide more than a global perspective on a staff member's performance. Thus, it is important that goals be set on an individual basis.

Goal-attainment scales provide the opportunity for the supervisor and the staff member to establish goals in order of priority, decide on clear indicators of progress and of attainment, and set time lines that are unique to each staff member and task. At appropriate times, the supervisor and staff member should update these lists by indicating what progress the staff member has made toward completion of the goals.

This strategy, with the written goal statement as the tool, is highly useful for working with professional staff and can be a valuable supplement to any appraisal process. Making comparisons between staff members is difficult, however, because each staff member will have different goals and the goals may not have comparable difficulty levels. Alternatives do exist, however, if you need to make comparisons. Competitive divers, for example, perform different dives that have been previously rated as to their level of difficulty; a diver's score is the judges' rating of the specific dive multiplied by the dive's difficulty level. It may not be possible or wise to aim for this level of precision in rating your staff's accomplishments, but it is quite likely that you already do this informally. You might think to yourself, "Mary organized and presented a series of five excellent how-to-study workshops for students, and that matches her goals. Harry only organized three workshops, two short of his goal, but one of them was on the difficult and sensitive topic of AIDS. Mary matched the goals we agreed on and Harry did not, but I believe that one of his goals was tougher to reach than Mary's."

Choosing Appraisal Strategies and Tools

No one approach or scale fits every situation. Each has its own strengths and weaknesses. Assessments that require substantial inferential judgments (such as narratives, rankings, or ratings based on personality traits) are usually weak on reliability and validity (see Chapter Eight for a discussion of these aspects of an appraisal system). These methods remain popular, however, because they are relatively easy to use. Most of us are familiar with them, they can be designed rather quickly, and they can be completed with ease by the raters. Rankings can be used with relatively little adaptation or calculation to determine the distribution of merit pay.

The behavioral assessment approach, with either observations or expectations as the rating premise, usually results in scales that have higher reliability and that predict future job performance better than ranking strategies or trait scales (DeVries, Morrison, Shullman, and Gerlach, 1981). These approaches can also provide information that is useful for staff development purposes. They tell you and the staff member what specific behavior needs to be changed.

Setting individual goals and appraising progress toward these goals provide the most feedback for planning sessions if you and your staff have specific projects in mind. This method also allows you and the staff member to establish goals for his or her professional development. However, the behavioral approaches and the individual-goal-setting approaches make comparisons among staff members difficult unless you assign the same weight for each behavior and for each goal accomplished. If you have different behavioral expectations for residence staff in some halls than in others, a uniform scale for appraising your residence hall staff will provide helpful information for a variety of purposes (such as deciding on training needs) but not necessarily for determining individual salary raises. If, on the other hand, the goals and their attainment are weighted, then such scales can be used for this purpose.

Conclusion

Ultimately, the relative effectiveness of any approach is determined by the persons who use it and its application. Chapter Four looks at issues related to implementing a performance appraisal system.

References

DeVries, D. L., Morrison, A. M., Shullman, S. L., and Gerlach, M. L. *Performance Appraisal on the Line.* New York: Wiley, 1981.
Equal Employment Opportunity Commission. "Adoption of Questions and Answers to Clarify and Provide a Common Interpretation of the Uniform

Guidelines on Employee Selection Procedures." *Federal Register*, 1979, *44*, 11996–12009.

Henderson, R. *Performance Appraisal: Theory to Practice*. Reston, Va.: Reston Publishing, 1980.

Kafry, D., Jacobs, R. R., and Zedeck, S. "Expectations of Behaviorally Anchored Rating Scales." *Personnel Psychology*, 1980, *33*, 595–640.

Latham, G. P., and Wexley, K. E. *Increasing Productivity Through Performance Appraisal*. Reading, Mass.: Addison-Wesley, 1981.

Deciding who provides appraisal information and ho
are to be trained are essential implementation steps.

Implementing
the Performance
Appraisal System

Scenario: John, a staff member of the health center at No
Nonsense University, opens his campus mail in late spring
to find a rating form. A form letter from the vice-president
for student affairs asks John to rate his boss, Dr. I. M.
Smart, on a dozen traits that cover both sides of the page,
and then he is to mail the rating form back in the self-
addressed envelope. John does not know whether or not the
rating form was sent to all staff members or how the information will be used or communicated to Dr. Smart. As
John reads the form, he finds few items that pertain to his
relationship with his boss, but he dutifully completes the
form by circling "average" or "above average" for all the
items, and mails it back.

Later in spring, Dr. Smart receives a note in the mail
from the vice-president with a summary of the ratings that
were completed by about half of her staff. The summary
says that her average rating was 4.78 on a five-point scale.
Her highest rating was on "reputation within the univer-

R. D. Brown. *Performance Appraisal as a Tool for Staff Development.*
New Directions for Student Services, no. 43. San Francisco: Jossey-Bass, Fall 1988.

) and her lowest rating was on "being accessible"
s1.24). An attached note from the vice-president says,
iese as you see fit. Good job."

n pressed, this vice-president could report that student affairs
ormance appraisal system that includes objective ratings and
has to the staff involved. This system is probably typical and proba-
feeeseful as a handkerchief in a driving rainstorm.
bly This chapter looks at three critical steps in implementing a per-
ance appraisal system at the organizational unit level: deciding who
uld provide appraisal information, providing a staff training program
appraisal, and testing the system.

Deciding Who Should Provide Appraisal Information

Several different groups can be involved in a staff member's performance appraisal: supervisors, peers, self, subordinates, students, and
external persons. Using responses from each group has its advantages
and disadvantages, as described in the following paragraphs.

Supervisors. The staff member's immediate supervisor is a logical
source of information about the staff member's performance. A strong
argument can be made for having the appraisal and the reward or pun-
ishment power in the same hands (Cummings and Schwab, 1982).
Middle-management supervisors often have difficulty dealing with such
role conflicts, however, particularly if they see themselves as teachers or
mentors as well as supervisors. As supervisors they may feel inadequate
because of lack of skill or training in appraisal, or they may feel uncomfortable because they fear alienating the staff and they do not wish to
play God.

Supervisors are vulnerable to several sources of error when making
ratings and personnel decisions. Their ratings can be contaminated
because of friendships, stereotypes, poorly understood standards, and
biases regarding personal characteristics of the staff member. Finding
deficiencies in friends is difficult to do. Supervisors may have formed
close friendships with staff members prior to assuming their supervisory
role. They may also tend to support the student affairs unit from which
they came. It is natural for a new dean of students to support counseling
center staff members if that is the unit in which she worked previously.
Or she may be more critical of staff from the counseling center because
she has firsthand knowledge of their weaknesses as well as of their
strengths. First impressions, whether correct or incorrect, can also serve
to establish stereotypes. Race, age, gender, and physical characteristics of
the staff member can also influence expectations and ratings.

Despite these potential sources of error or bias, supervisors should have performance appraisal responsibilities, and they should be a major source of appraisal information.

Colleagues. Assuming that coworkers have knowledge about the performance of other staff members, information collected from colleagues can be useful if there is general trust throughout the staff, a good environment for sharing, and a noncompetitive reward system (Kane and Lawler, 1978). If these conditions do not exist, using peer ratings can create problems. Staff may fear that their anonymity will be violated and that they may thus lose a friend. Close rivalries or friendships can bias appraisals. Despite being in similar positions or in the same unit, staff members may not know the particular constraints and circumstances affecting their colleagues' work. A residence director in one hall, for example, may not know the specific historical background of the problems in another hall. A career development center director may not have an understanding of the caseload limitations of staff in the psychological services center. Colleague feedback can be most useful when appraisals provide information for staff development purposes, but numerous difficulties can arise if this source of information is used for salary determinations.

Self. Self appraisal is inevitable. Everyone has implicit, if not explicit, professional goals, and, despite whatever self-deception may exist, everyone makes judgments about his or her job effectiveness. Staff members make informal judgments about their individual performance throughout the year. It may take the form of noting that a leadership program seemed to work or it did not, as judged by student comments. It may be sensing that a staff problem-solving session went better or worse than expected. It may also involve comparing oneself with other staff members, as in the thought that "I carry as heavy a load as anyone on the staff." Self-evaluation is a constant and natural process, but how useful is self-evaluation in a performance appraisal system?

A comprehensive self-rating tool can provide staff members with helpful reminders of the skills and behaviors they must work on. A supervisor could use a collection of anonymous self-ratings as a needs assessment for planning future staff development programs. Formal self-appraisals provided in writing or during interviews with supervisors are helpful if the focus is on professional development and the purpose is to promote personal growth. Using self-appraisal information for determining salary increases or deciding on promotions is inappropriate, but, when self-appraisal is tied to a self-improvement effort, the process is usually more satisfying to management and staff and also usually results in more motivated staff members.

Self-appraisal information can be obtained and used in several ways within a developmental framework. The staff member can be asked to rate himself or herself on the same characteristics and job performance dimensions that colleagues or a supervisor use. Comparisons of self-ratings to peer ratings can be highly informative. This is particularly true for dimensions related to interpersonal skills and communications. Staff members can be unaware of the impact of their behavior on others.

Self-appraisals can be most effective if combined with a mentoring or coaching support system. Staff should not be expected to make their own interpretations of their appraisals without training or support. They are likely to be biased positively toward themselves, but they can also underestimate their potential and overestimate what they can accomplish during a specified time period. A mentoring system can help infuse the appropriate balance of realism into their expectations of themselves.

Subordinates. Do you have residence hall staff rate the performance of hall directors? Should hall directors rate the performance of the residence hall director? Should the director rate the performance of his or her division head? Appraisal information from subordinate staff provides useful information about how well staff members communicate job knowledge, how much interest they show in their own staff, and how well they coordinate their staff in their area of responsibility.

Staff members who rate their superior are likely to respond on the basis of whether or not their own needs have been met. Their responses reflect how well they believe they have been supervised, how quickly the supervisor has responded to requests, and how well they believe the supervisor has represented the unit's concerns to other administrators. This can be useful information, but it is not a substitute for information that tells us whether or not the overall needs of the unit were met. Individual staff members may have interests and needs that cannot be met without conflicting with the interests of other staff members so that the supervisor cannot possibly meet everyone's needs. One staff member may want more student worker support, for example, but there is only so much to go around. Two staff members may have contrasting concepts for a new student orientation program, but only one program can be supported and implemented.

Appraisal feedback from subordinates should not be ignored, but careful thought needs to go into deciding what information should be collected and how it is used. What may be important, for example, is not whether or not a staff member believes that her good idea was rejected but the process that was used to make that decision. Does she believe her idea was given a fair hearing? Does she believe favoritism was involved? Other important dimensions on which subordinate staff can provide useful information include how clear their own responsibilities are to them, how adequate their training and supervision has been, and how well they perceive their concerns to be represented to other administrators.

Much of the information obtained from subordinates will come in the form of opinions and attitudes. This information can provide a sense of the morale within the unit and an indicator of the respect that the staff has for their supervisor. When possible, however, opinions and attitude data should be supported by behavioral feedback.

Here are a few examples of items that ask for behavioral information:

1. How often in the past two months did your supervisor tell you that he or she had communicated your and other staff members' concerns to other administrators? (Response categories could range from "never" to "frequently," or the item could be open-ended.)

2. How often in the past two months, either in a meeting with other staff or in a private conversation, did your supervisor ask for your ideas on how to improve a program or solve a problem? (Response categories could range from "never" to "frequently," or the item could be open-ended. This question could be divided into two parts: group settings, such as staff meetings, and private settings.)

3. How often is staff input sought for determining topics for staff development programs? (Response categories could range from "never" to "always.")

4. How comfortable do you feel about consulting your supervisor when you have the following difficulties? (This question would be followed by such topics as dealing with a discipline problem, answering a parental concern, or coping with a disagreeable staff colleague, and response categories would range from "very comfortable" to "very uncomfortable." This format could be combined with another question asking respondents to indicate how frequently they actually discussed these concerns with their supervisor. Also, respondents could be asked to provide the reason for their individual answers.)

Key demographic characteristics of staff members can be helpful information to have when interpreting the results of the ratings. Comparing responses of persons of different genders, for example, might help sort out biases or different interpersonal styles and needs that influence relationships between staff and their supervisors. Knowing whether or not the responses are from relatively new or from experienced professionals could also be useful. Anonymity, however, must be guaranteed in the process of collecting and using the information. If the staff is small enough so that information on gender and years on the job make it possible to identify or to make a good guess about who the respondent is, then this information should not be collected.

Students. Do you have residence hall students rate the performance of floor assistants and the director? For many, if not most, student affairs positions, how students feel about the services and programs provided is an important appraisal consideration. Consumer feedback is, in most instances, the ultimate appraisal feedback, and certainly for student services the feedback from students is essential. Be sure to distinguish, however, between feedback that helps program planning from feedback that helps appraise individual staff. A campus activities director may find appraisal feedback from student organization leaders helpful in determining the effectiveness of his program even though the responses are confidential and he is not able to identify what staff member the respondent worked with during the year. A counseling center director, on the other hand, might find it useful to report total client satisfaction scores for her center and at the same time be able to sort out the satisfaction scores counselor by counselor. If the pool of respondents is large enough, she might be able to compare the satisfaction of vocational-choice clients to that of personal-problem clients by counselor. This could be helpful feedback to the counselor and provide an indication of where strengths and weaknesses exist. Again, it is essential to guarantee confidentiality to the student respondents, and this is conveyed best by making sure that the responses are anonymous.

Appropriate use of student appraisal feedback by student affairs units on campus could provide a model for faculty and other staff within the higher education community. Behavioral indicators are again an essential element of good appraisals. Knowing that students were satisfied with the services provided is good information, but it is essential to know whether students changed their behavior or not. Did the undecided student eventually make a decision? Did the registering student enroll in the appropriate courses? Did the student organization leader master key leadership skills? These outcome indicators are particularly useful for program appraisal as opposed to performance appraisal, but they should be kept in mind for both uses (Brown and Sanstead, 1982).

External Persons. Persons outside the unit can provide appraisal information when you need to call on expertise that is not available within your unit or when objectivity is particularly necessary. Outsiders will know less about the circumstances surrounding the work environment, and this has both advantages and disadvantages. External persons are less likely to be influenced by biases due to a history of relationships with the individuals, and they may have insights into situations not possible for those directly involved. This also means, however, that they are less likely to be aware of possible mitigating circumstances. An outsider, for example, may be unaware that the counseling center and general advising staffs were recently combined and that the advising staff is still upset about this merger and resists the leadership of the counseling center director. On the other hand, staff might be more open to describing their concerns to an outsider than to someone internal to the unit or the campus.

Among a comfortable, collegial staff, it might be possible to have directors serve as data collectors and appraisers for each other. Much could be learned. This works best for an appraisal designed exclusively for professional development. In a competitive working environment, it is best to have the appraiser be someone external to student affairs or to the campus. For self-improvement purposes, directors might invite colleagues from other institutions to visit their campus and to conduct an on-site appraisal of their performance. This takes courage, but it can be quite useful. This process will take more time and money and is probably most cost effective for appraising senior staff. Feedback in one form or another should be given to the staff member as well as to the supervisor.

No single performance rater is better than the immediate supervisor, though multiple ratings may be best (DeVries, Morrison, Shullman, and Gerlach, 1981). Getting input from several sources provides a larger data base for decision making. This also makes it possible to determine the reliability of the ratings by correlating the ratings of one group to those of another group. If the ratings from multiple sources agree, you can feel reasonably comfortable about the reliability of the ratings. If, however, there is disagreement and the ratings vary dramatically, you must make decisions about what information is accurate. If the ratings within one group (such as students) are consistent, but these are different than the ratings of another group (such as coworkers), then it is apparent that the staff member being rated is perceived and perhaps behaves differently with students than with coworkers. If the ratings within one group are consistent except for one or two respondents out of twenty, then you must make a judgment as to whether or not those disparate ratings should be ignored because they are either not accurate or not representative of the typical behavior of the staff person being rated.

Training Staff in Performance Appraisal

A performance appraisal system can be no better than the persons using it. The best observational rating form can be misused by raters. The best data-gathering system can lose its value when those data are improperly reported. Student affairs staffs are usually experienced program planners and staff trainers. You would not, for example, think of having staff participate in a recently developed student orientation program without a staff training program. But how often do student affairs administrators put a performance appraisal rating form in the campus mail with instructions only on how to mail it back? Or how often do administrators assume that staff who have supervisory responsibilities know how to conduct an appraisal interview?

Staff should be trained in how to conduct performance appraisals and in how to be appraised. They need to be trained to give appraisals and to receive appraisals. Let us look first at the training necessary to conduct performance appraisals.

Training Staff in Conducting Appraisals. You must attend to the content of the training and to the process. The content of the training program should include: (1) organizational goals, the purposes of the appraisal, and how these fit together; (2) measuring instruments, standards, and procedures; (3) possible appraisal errors; and (4) appraisal interviews. Staff need to understand the philosophy and objectives of the organizational unit and the philosophy and objectives of the appraisal system. What are the objectives of the student affairs unit, and how does the appraisal process fit into those goals? What is the purpose of the appraisal system? What methods will be used in the appraisal process? Answers to these questions will help staff understand how performance appraisal can help them and can help the unit reach its objectives.

If the appraisal tools, such as rating scales, have already been developed, the tools can be described and staff can practice making ratings and interpreting rating results. Simulation exercises that include brief descriptions of work behavior and require participants to rate the behavior are excellent ways to arrive at shared meanings of descriptive ratings. Depending on the time available, this could also be an opportunity to devise new forms or revise current forms. Describe the major sources of error in making ratings and how these can be prevented (the next section in this chapter covers rating errors). Staff should have the opportunity to clarify the meaning of rating scale descriptors (for example, what the difference is between "frequently" and "almost always"). Seeing the ratings that others give to the same work behavior can help reduce rating errors. For staff who will be interviewing their subordinates, different interviewing strategies can be demonstrated and practiced. If the assessment process includes a professional development objective, staff should become familiar with methods to implement this objective. How do you develop a performance improvement plan? How do you coach or mentor your subordinate?

Choosing a Training Format. A lecture or formal presentation format is not as effective as group discussion and practice (Spool, 1978). Staff members need presentations on the basics of performance appraisal, but they also need practice, feedback on how they did, and guidance as to how they might improve. A good training program will include: (1) modeling of appropriate behavior through fishbowl exercises or videotape presentations, (2) individual practice, (3) feedback on how well each person is doing, and (4) an opportunity to apply the knowledge in increasingly realistic and complex situations. Too often modeling presentations or exercises use only straightforward situations without progressing to more complex situations and decisions. As a result, staff members understand the basic intent but find it difficult to apply the concepts in a real-world setting.

Understanding Common Rating Errors. Rating forms promise to remain an integral part of performance appraisal, and the concepts involved in completing them accurately apply to appraisal judgments in many different contexts. It is essential, therefore, that anyone completing or interpreting ratings be familiar with sources of error and how to prevent them. Training staff to be alert to these errors should be an important module of any staff training program.

A rating error is the difference between the judgment recorded on a form, scale, or other procedure about a person's performance and an accurate assessment of that person's performance. The error can be due to honest mistaken judgment, bias or prejudice, lack of information, or other extraneous influences. Rating errors made on a rating form during or right after an observational process or on an end-of-the-year rating form are similar. The following paragraphs describe some common types of errors.

The *contrast effect* is the tendency to evaluate a person relative to other individuals rather than relative to the job requirements. This is frequently influenced by the order in which individuals are rated. Rating an extremely superior or extremely poor performer first is likely to influence the ratings of the rest of the individuals. If you have just rated a super performer, the next person's performance will look quite modest by comparison, and, even though his or her performance was average, you may have a tendency to rate it lower than you would otherwise. On the other hand, average performers may get a higher rating than merited if their ratings take place just after you have rated the lowest person on the staff.

Sometimes administrators suggest or raters mistakenly believe that you cannot rate everyone high and therefore an allotment system is necessary—something like grading on a normal curve. You may be asked to report the names of the top 10 percent of your staff or the top third. At first this seems like a logical request, but there can be problems. Does the staff break out neatly into these divisions? Is there a significant and justifiable difference between the staff members on both sides of the cutoffs, between the last person that makes it into the top 10 percent and the next person who did not make it? Seldom are appraisal processes that precise, and seldom do the staff performances fall neatly into these categories. Making decisions about staff salaries on the basis of something like an allotment system will probably not be viewed positively by the courts (Latham and Wexley, 1981).

Comparing individuals when making ratings (notice the distinction between ranking persons from top to bottom and rating them on job performance) either intentionally or unintentionally is inappropriate. Staff members should be appraised on the basis of how well they do their jobs and not on how they compare to others. Later it may be necessary and appropriate to rank staff, but not when making ratings.

Contrast errors can be avoided by rating as many staff members at

a time as possible, making sure the ratings are tied to the job requirements and standards, and rating the staff members in a random order.

The *halo, horn, recency,* and *spillover effects* involve inappropriately generalizing from one aspect of a person's job performance to
other aspects. For example, a residence life director sees a staff member as
a highly effective and well-organized program planner. This is a staff
member who can be counted on to carry out an effective program from
design to implementation. This perception can easily influence the residence life director's ratings of that staff member on other job dimensions.
It is quite likely that this staff member will be rated high on all other
performance measures.

The horn effect is close to the opposite, rating a staff member low
on all job performance dimensions because of one characteristic. A staff
member who is continually late for staff meetings and always requires
updating on what happened during the meeting could prompt a rater to
give lower ratings on several other job performance dimensions just
because he has become an annoyance.

Somewhat similar to the halo effect are the recency and spillover
effects—letting the staff member's most recent behavior or some past
behavior significantly influence a rating on current behavior. Rating a
staff member low at the end of a six-month rating period because he
conducted a poor staff meeting last week is an example of a recency
effect. Rating a staff member low because of an alcohol problem that
happened a year ago is an example of a spillover effect. Raters must ask
themselves whether or not the behavior that is influencing the specific
rating is representative of the staff member's job behavior for the full
period that the rating is intended to cover.

Halo, horn, and recency errors can be avoided by using rating
scales that have primarily behavioral items. Trait-scales are particularly
vulnerable to halo or horn effects. If a person is seen as odd, perhaps
frequently contrary, or, by contrast, as highly dependable, the ratings are
susceptible to the halo or horn effect. Susan always asks tough, direct,
and what appear at times to be hostile questions at staff meetings. This
may appropriately affect the rating of her "cooperativeness." But should
it also influence the rating of her "dependability" and "initiative?" It
might. Bill always has his reports or responses to requests for information
in well before deadlines. His ratings on "promptness" or "dependability"
should be high, but should his ratings on "approachableness" or on the
quality of his reports also be high? A rating scale that asks you to indicate
whether or not "reports provide specific suggestions for next steps" or
"meeting agendas are available prior to the meeting date" is less susceptible to halo or horn effects than one that asks you to indicate whether or
not a staff member is "organized."

It is tempting to find out how others have rated a person before you make your ratings, but this is not appropriate. If you are responsible for collating feedback on a staff member, do your own rating of the individual before tabulating the results from others. When you put all of the information together, the responses from others may appropriately influence your final judgment, but your initial ratings should be independent.

The *similar-to-me effect* is due to the natural tendency to like people who are similar—people who have similar interests, backgrounds, and goals. Knowing that a staff member shares your interest in golf, jogging, or jazzercize often means that you believe he or she cannot be all bad. Having similar job strengths such as a liking for details or for planning ahead can also influence performance ratings.

Again, a clear, behavioral job description and a job-related rating scale can help prevent this error. Also, having multiple raters increases the possibility that there will be a balance of backgrounds, interests, and attitudes reflected in the ratings.

When raters demonstrate *directional biases*, they give similar ratings to all staff members, such as rating all near the middle (a central tendency), giving everyone low ratings (a negative tendency), or giving everyone high ratings (leniency). The central tendency pattern is common and represents an easy escape for the rater who does not wish to make appraisal judgments. The resulting ratings have little value for discriminating among staff. Giving continually low or high ratings is no better. Constant low ratings result in staff dislike of the process and low morale; constant high ratings result in less respect for the process and cynicism when high ratings do not result in equally high salary increases.

Using a rating form that has an even number of response categories with no middle or average (for example "superior," "above average," "below average," and "inadequate") forces the rater to get off the fence and to rate a person as relatively low or relatively high. Some staff members and their performances, however, are average, and thus such a scale does not represent reality. Rating-scale experts are divided as to whether to use an even or an odd number of response categories, but, since it is possible to be undecided or neutral, it seems reasonable that a middle response be provided.

The errors described here are impossible to avoid completely, but there are guidelines to help reduce the frequency and impact of such errors: First, avoiding trait scales is important. Working hard to make the rating or observational scales as behavioral as possible is critical to having a good performance appraisal process. Behavioral scales are more valid and reliable whether used for salary and promotion decisions or for staff development purposes. Behavioral scales are essential if you hope to provide useful feedback to staff. Telling a staff member she is viewed as "uncooperative" or "undependable" is not nearly as helpful as telling her that she was not available when she should have been to help her subordinates and that her reports have been repeatedly late. Staff training in performance appraisal will also help reduce errors and improve the system.

Training Staff in Being Appraised. The most neglected persons in the training process are the staff members who are being appraised. What should they know about the performance appraisal system and how should they be trained? Preparing staff members to be appraised can have several benefits. If they are to be active participants in the design and implementation of an appraisal system, then the more they know beforehand about the purposes of the system, the more valuable and relevant their input is likely to be. They can also serve as knowledgeable monitors of the appraisal system if they know how it is supposed to work. They can, for example, provide feedback on the implementation itself: What took place during the planning session? What follow-up took place? What level of support did they have?

Staff training should provide them with as much information about the system as possible, and give them practice in being appraised, particularly in goal-setting and appraisal interviews. Staff should have copies of their job descriptions and ample opportunity to go over them with their supervisors. They should have a clear understanding of what tasks they are expected to perform and what the standards are for success. They should also know how and when evaluative data will be collected. Will they be observed? Will their students be surveyed? Will their own staffs be asked to rate their job performance? What will the rating scales look like? Will some criteria have more weight than others? If the staff are involved in designing and implementing the appraisal system, their knowledge of the process should be adequate. Not all staff will be involved in the planning, but they must be aware of the system.

Chapter Six discusses the appraisal interview from the perspective of the interviewer, but staff could also benefit from training in how to be a good interviewee. Staff need to recognize that it is important for them to be appropriately assertive in the interview process. When the focus of the interview is on goal-setting, they should be sure they understand what the goals are, comment directly on whether they see the goals and the time-lines as realistic, and make sure they understand what the next steps are. When the interview focuses on assessment of what has happened during the year, staff need to know what information they should provide, how to organize and present it, how to ensure that the interview provides them with accurate feedback on the quality of their performance, and how to ensure that the information is useful to them in determining ways to improve their performance.

The format for this training may range from participation in the planning of the appraisal system, knowing what their supervisor is expected to do, to practice in being interviewed through simulation and role-playing exercises. By knowing what their supervisors are expected to do (for example, the kind of feedback supervisors are expected to provide), staff can feel more comfortable in asserting their needs for that feedback when it is not forthcoming. If role-playing exercises or video-taped simulations are used to train directors in conducting appraisal interviews, these same exercises or simulations can also be used for training staff to be interviewed. The focus becomes the behavior of the interviewee rather than the interviewer.

Training experiences like these are done best in group settings—for example large groups that then break down into small groups for discussion and small group exercises. Providing the training sessions for staff from different student affairs units provides the opportunity for the cross-fertilization of ideas and also possibly prevents one director from providing a narrow or limiting view of which behavior is appropriate for the staff member.

Many staff members have staffs of their own and some will eventually have administrative positions. The experience and insights gained from being appraised unfortunately do not automatically lead to different behaviors when those same staff members become supervisors. Training in performance appraisal techniques and exposure to what a good performance appraisal system is like, however, should raise the level of what staff members expect from their supervisors and provide them with role models should they someday be supervisors themselves.

If the appraisal process is a good system, then the behavior of the staff member being appraised is a crucial link in the system. It is a link that has too often been neglected. A good performance appraisal system provides training for all those who will be responding to questionnaires or rating forms. It also provides training and practice in the interview techniques associated with performance appraisals. Chapter Six discusses interview strategies in more detail.

Pilot Testing the Appraisal System

Edison tried hundreds of different materials as potential filaments before he discovered the right one for the electric light bulb. No one builds any technological system today without pilot testing components separately and then testing the entire system in small stages. A new performance appraisal system should be phased in rather than implemented in one fell swoop throughout the unit. There are two ways to phase in the system: Use one unit as a pilot site, or use one staff level. If the system is going to be implemented across all student services units and you want to pilot it within one unit, select a unit that is most representative and in which you believe it has the best opportunity to be successful. In this way, you will have a chance to debug the system before expanding it to other units.

Piloting the system first with the top level of management is another successful strategy. Directors and others at similar levels can be role models for the rest of the staff and can encourage their own staff to implement variations in the system at their level. These two strategies can be combined by pilot testing the system with senior staff and simultaneously, within one student affairs unit.

Conclusion

You can obtain useful appraisal information from a variety of internal and external sources. Staff need to be involved in the planning of the system and properly informed or trained if the appraisal information they provide is going to suit your purposes. Remember that you are not tightening the screws on a piece of machinery that you will not have to look at again for another twenty years. You are creating a system that needs constant attention and requires continual minor and major adjustments. The events described in Figure 1 in Chapter Two do not end when the full system is in place; rather, they start all over again.

References

Brown, R. D., and Sanstead, M. "Using Evaluations to Make Decisions About Academic Advising Programs." In R. B. Winston, Jr., S. C. Ender, and T. K. Miller (eds.), *Developmental Approaches to Academic Advising*. New Directions for Student Services, no. 17. San Francisco: Jossey-Bass, 1982.

Cummings, L. L., and Schwab, D. P. "Who Evaluates?" In L. S. Baird, R. W. Beatty, and C. E. Schneier (eds.), *The Performance Appraisal Sourcebook*. Amherst, Mass.: Human Resources Development Press, 1982.

DeVries, D. L., Morrison, A. M., Shullman, S. L., and Gerlach, M. L. *Performance Appraisal on the Line*. New York: Wiley, 1981.

Kane, J. S., and Lawler, E. E., III. "Method of Peer Assessment." *Psychological Bulletin*, 1978, *85*, 555–586.

Latham, G. P., and Wexley, K. E. *Increasing Productivity Through Performance Appraisal*. Reading, Mass.: Addison-Wesley, 1981.

Spool, M. D. "Training Programs for Observers of Behaviors: A Review." *Personnel Psychology*, 1978, *31*, 879–888.

*Helping staff members set goals and tying these to
student affairs unit goals are essential elements of a
performance appraisal system.*

Setting Goals in Performance
Appraisal Interviews

Scenario: Jonathan, a financial aid staff member, has just
finished his end-of-the-year annual review with his supervisor. As it has been for several years, the time was divided
almost equally between light chitchat and discussion of
activities and crises that took place during the past year.
Just when the conversation began to turn toward the
future—what should be done differently next year—the
hour was up. Each agreed that they would meet again soon,
or early in the fall at the latest, to discuss goals for the next
year. Jonathan recalls as he leaves the meeting that this
pattern has been almost identical for three years. They have
never held a meeting to discuss goals and plans for the
year. The start of a new year is always a busy time for
financial aid offices. Jonathan vows that, on his own initiative, he will schedule such a meeting. Then he remembers
that he made the same vow last year.

Good performance appraisal systems include goal-setting sessions
with individual staff members (Olson, 1981). Annual reviews have
become a traditional and perhaps somewhat grudgingly accepted part of

R. D. Brown. *Performance Appraisal as a Tool for Staff Development.*
New Directions for Student Services, no. 43. San Francisco: Jossey-Bass, Fall 1988.

most student affairs systems. Necessary decisions related to salary, merit pay, and promotions usually dictate a review process. Beginning-of-the-year planning and goal-setting sessions are also seen as necessary, but there is extensive slippage in their occurrence (Lazer and Wikstrom, 1977). Many management-by-objectives systems deteriorate into primarily assessment-by-objectives without the preliminary essential steps of planning, setting goals, and conducting interim reviews.

Effective goal setting and follow-up could easily represent 80 percent of an effective performance appraisal system; these activities are probably underrepresented in most student affairs appraisal systems. This chapter presents guidelines for working with staff in setting goals, assessing progress, and making appropriate changes.

Ensure That Goals Are Specific

Objectives should be specific so that you and the staff member clearly understand what is to be accomplished. When it is difficult to be precise, provide a range. Here are examples of specific goals: (1) Staff member will organize and coordinate the implementation of three to five residence hall programs with at least one based on a formal needs assessment of resident interests and concerns; (2) staff member will consult with the student judicial board in planning workshop on moral development and board decisions; and (3) staff member will train ten to fifteen undergraduate paraprofessionals who will provide half-day workshops on study techniques and test anxiety.

At first, the supervisor and the staff member will have to estimate what goals will be realistic. The goals can always be changed or renegotiated, but the specificity provides the staff member with clear expectations about what is to be accomplished.

Make Goals Measurable

Ideally, goals should be expressed in a measurable form. Two extreme opinions exist on this issue: One says that, if you cannot measure the goal, then the goal is not worth pursuing. One example of a goal that is difficult to measure would be: Director will be open to new ideas from staff members. The other position holds strongly that no worthwhile goals are measurable and that trying too hard to do so results in trivial goals. An example of a trivial goal would be: "Staff member spends at least five minutes per week with each student assistant." It is difficult to develop measurable goals for high-level management or supervisory positions. Good leadership, such as that needed to assist a staff in working through a difficult short-handed period after several retirements and transfers, is not easy to measure with precision. As a result, goal statements often remain vague.

When writing goal statements for yourself or for others, continually ask what the behavior would be that exemplifies accomplishment of each goal. Behavioral definitions of good leadership, for example, might include process goals, such as training staff or conducting joint projects with other student affairs units. If a staff director behaves as you expect a good leader to behave, then he or she is probably a good leader.

The next step, another difficult one, is to determine what the criteria are for success. What if a director behaves like a good leader—that is, she performs all the expected behaviors—but she performs them at a low level? What if a director has a staff training program and sponsors joint projects with other student affairs units but does so at a very minimal level? Completion of these tasks does not automatically provide an indication of how well they were performed. Criteria for what represents success in training staff or participating in cooperative projects with other units need to be defined. Though it will take work, it is possible to develop a list of behavioral descriptions that typify good leadership (for example, obtains staff consensus, determines staff needs, engages in long-range planning).

Set Behavior Goals for Individuals and Outcome Goals for Units

Business and industry managers set outcome goals for individuals and units. Sales and marketing personnel are expected to sell so many products or ads, and the outcome is measured in terms of sales volume, often in dollar amounts. In production, the number of items constructed becomes the performance measure for individuals and units. Are the same behavioral assessments appropriate in an educational setting? Should teachers be appraised on the basis of what their students learn? Should residence hall directors be appraised on the grade-point average of their residents?

In student affairs, for the most part, behavior goals should be established for individual staff members, and outcome goals should be established for units within student affairs. Counseling center staff members, for example, can be accountable for presenting workshops on study skills and being accessible to help individual students, but they should not be accountable for the grade point or attrition rate of students. Housing staff can be accountable for sponsoring an alcohol awareness activity and enforcing regulations regarding drinking behavior but not for the number of students who abuse alcohol outside the residence hall. Campus activities staff can be responsible for providing advice for student organizations that are planning social activities but not for the ultimate success of those activities.

It is sometimes difficult to separate the outcomes (such as the number of students caught drinking in a residence hall) from the process (alcohol education programming), and administrators often reward staff on the basis of outcome as well as process. It is also easy to focus on the wrong outcome. The staff member, for example, working with a campus organization that loses money on a sponsored event is vulnerable to having that loss rub off on him as an indicator of his advising skills. Probably everyone involved would have felt better had the event made money or broken even. But calling the effort a failure is a mistake because this does not consider the educational outcomes; it considers only the monetary outcomes.

You and your staff may want to discuss this issue further. For what outcomes or processes should staff be held accountable? Why should the focus be on process expectations rather than on product outcomes? There are several reasons: First, staff should not be responsible for circumstances or actions they cannot control. They can manage and control their own behavior but not the behavior of students. Second, if they are to serve in educational developmental roles, they must permit students to make mistakes. Third, outcomes in student services are the result of a highly complex series of interactions and are influenced by other staff members' performances as well as by that of the individual staff member being evaluated. And, finally, the process is often as important as the product. Whether or not the planned social activity of a campus organization comes off without a hitch is probably less important than whether or not the student leaders organizing the activity learned something about planning during the process.

In many instances, good performance on the behavioral expectations also results in good outcomes. If residence hall staff members perform up to expectations, it is natural to expect that the hall will be a good educational and living environment for students, which is, after all, the ultimate goal of the residence hall staff. Evidence of their accomplishment of that objective includes measures of student satisfaction, requests to return to the hall next year, attrition rates, and grade-point averages as well as other indicators. The goals of individual staff members within the residence hall include providing the programs, resources, and consultation that lead toward these residence hall unit objectives.

Set the Goals Jointly

Staff need to participate in setting goals for themselves and for their contributions toward the unit's objectives. Often this participation results in higher goals than if the administrator alone set the goals. You usually do not need to worry about the mutually set goals being too low. Staff participation in any phase of the performance appraisal process works best if participation is expected throughout the entire process and not just for one step or for one component. If a campus activities staff has no input into developing job descriptions or establishing criteria for successful work, it may be a shock to them to be asked to set their personal goals. Do not expect your staff, individually or collectively, to participate effectively in goal-setting activities if you do not involve them in any other decisions. Experience in working together in collaborative relationships and trust in each other are essential if mutual goal setting is going to be effective.

Professional staff often have several agendas for setting goals. These will vary with their own history within their unit or within the particular institution. Long-term staff members in a career development center may wish to maintain the status quo, whereas new staff members may want to make changes based on their more recent training. Both may have broader career aspirations that aim to enhance their stature and perhaps mobility within the profession. These professional goals need to be considered. However, it is equally important to consider the match of the individual staff member's goals and those of the student affairs unit. Do the staff member's goals facilitate the accomplishment of the unit's goals? If a counseling center staff member wants to maintain a heavy client load of married couples and complete an involved and extensive research project for publication, the counseling center director has to consider how well this fits into the center's overall objectives, which may focus more on outreach and the needs of students indecisive about their careers. Mutually setting goals does not mean capitulation of unit goals to the professional goals of staff members any more than it means forcing staff to mold themselves entirely to the unit's goals. A negotiated balance is needed, and it is more appropriate to arrive at this during the goal-setting period than during the end-of-the-year appraisal session.

Set Time Lines

Have a time line for every goal. Goals that are vague and have no time line will usually remain little more than fantasies with remote possibilities of completion. A goal that says that the staff member will gather information about substance abuse on campus may lead to a few quick phone calls to the health center or counseling center, an intensive and extensive survey of students that will take months to complete, or it may lead to no action because the staff member remembers that these suggestions were never followed up after past sessions. On the other hand, a goal that says the staff member will coordinate a committee with representatives from the health center and counseling center that will survey a random sample of students with a report due by April provides the staff member with clear expectations as to what needs to be done and when.

The time lines should be renegotiable as events and circumstances demand, but having time lines provides all involved with a sense of the importance of the goal and also a method for setting priorities.

Establish Challenging but Realistic Goals

Staff grow through being challenged; they stagnate when expectations are too low. Challenge has been the cornerstone of developmental theory, and it applies to staff development as well as to student development (Sanford, 1962). Research in a variety of work settings repeatedly supports the value of setting specific goals as contrasted to telling staff to "do your best" (Latham and Wexley, 1981).

Good staff members are likely to set goals that are too high. They may be trying to impress you, but they also probably have too many goals and too high expectations of themselves. A good supervisor will help staff keep their goals realistic. This will help staff morale; it is always better to accomplish a bit more than you intended than to accomplish less than you intended. It is also likely to reduce staff burnout. Goals should be high but not unrealistic. Goals that are too high result in discouragement, depression, and ultimately less effort.

Provide Support

For challenge to result in effective improvement, it must be accompanied by sufficient support. In staff relations, this needs to be more than promises of standing behind staff members or providing a safety net if their effort to meet the challenges are unsuccessful. Goals and support for each staff member must be as explicit as possible. Support can take different forms. It might include promising availability: "I will be available as often as you want to discuss the project," or "Let's schedule regular meetings to continue our discussion of this project." It could mean providing help from or consulting with members of other staffs: "I will check with the counseling center director to see how many staff could participate in your staff training projects." Or it could mean providing logistical, clerical support: "I can make my secretary available for any typing you need done," or "I can get you a work-study student to help you with the xeroxing and collating of materials."

Responding creatively to new challenges requires taking risks and often necessitates going beyond what is already being done or doing something different from what is currently being done. The staff member should know that the supervisor supports this stretching with his or her encouragement, consultation time, and logistical support. Staying with the project demonstrates your commitment to the specific goal and reflects the importance of the project to you.

Have an Action Plan

Work with the staff member on how the goals are going to be accomplished. The amount of detail you go into here may depend on the nature of the tasks and the position of the person you are supervising. For an important or highly involved project or with a new staff member, you might ask the staff member to develop an action plan and submit it to you for review and further discussion. You are modeling appropriate planning behavior that includes setting goals. Good goal-setting techniques involve establishing milestones, setting time lines, and designating indicators that let you know when you have reached your goal. Make sure you indicate what your next step will be as the supervisor and what next step the staff member needs to take. You might make a note: "By Tuesday, I will contact the counseling center director about the staff she has available to work on this with you and get that information to you. In the meantime, you can check with the student government president about how long it will take to have a student representative appointed to the planning group."

Include Personal Development Plans

Every staff member's plan should include plans for professional growth. The personal development plans can range from gaining new knowledge (such as learning about budget processes) or new skills (such as learning stress reduction strategies) to participating in research or appraisal projects. Try to fit them into the regular work plan. Help the staff member establish an individual goal that will accomplish a unit goal and will also provide the staff member an opportunity to grow. For instance, after the staff member has mastered several stress reduction strategies, he or she could provide a stress reduction workshop for other staff members or students. Participation in student affairs research team projects could provide the staff member with an opportunity to gain new skills at the same time that she contributes to the unit's goals.

Like other performance goals, personal growth goals should be specific and realistic. The goals should be aimed at adding new knowledge, skills, or new ways of looking at oneself. A staff member's personal growth goal might be developing new strategies for coping with stress for himself as well as learning how to help students cope. It is important for staff to realize that, unless they care for themselves as total persons, they are unlikely to be totally effective in helping students.

If you cannot promise a promotion based on attainment of new skills, be careful not to imply that a promotion follows. A vital key to staff satisfaction is being able to use current skills and gain new ones. Providing the opportunity for self-development may be an insufficient reward in and of itself, but it is an important one. It may take time and effort to educate the staff and gain their trust in your expectations for self-development. Not all staff will immediately feel comfortable or practiced in defining and setting goals for their own personal growth.

Conduct Follow-Up Interviews

The goal-setting phase of the performance appraisal process is most frequently followed up by the end-of-the-year interview with no formal or informal meeting in between. This is insufficient. The usual excuse for the lack of interim meetings is that there is no time. Probably an equally influencing reason, but one not articulated, is that the administrator dislikes the process sufficiently to delay or avoid further meetings as much as possible.

You will be observing and interacting with the staff regularly throughout the year, but your performance appraisal system should include regular follow-up sessions between the goal-setting and the appraisal interviews. You need to review progress, discuss and resolve problems, and make whatever changes are advisable. In rocket trips to the moon, a midcourse correction maneuver fine-tunes the navigational system on the basis of fuel and telemetry projections. It is unfortunate that more administrators do not see the value of such midcourse corrections for student affairs staff development plans.

Interim meetings provide opportunities for doing formally what you hope to be doing continuously: encouraging staff, checking progress, troubleshooting, and gathering staff input on how well certain projects and their work in general are going. Feedback is essential to goal attainment. Long-distance runners benefit from knowing how far they have run, how far they have to go, and what their pace is. This feedback provides information for them to adjust their pace and motivates them to maintain their current pace or go faster. You like to believe you are providing your staff feedback regularly on an informal basis, but paths do not always cross and it is easy to get distracted.

Schedule follow-up sessions with all staff, not just those on new projects or those who are having problems. Even the most accomplished staff member can feel slighted if you are spending all your time with staff who are floundering. A developmental approach to performance appraisal necessitates that you spend an appropriate amount of time with staff who are succeeding as well as with staff who are in trouble. Focusing all your time on crises and troubled staff can result in a flat performance profile across the staff: No staff member will be outstanding. The bright, eager, and innovating staff members need challenge and support in their planning and performing as well as the average, bored, and stagnant staff members.

Make your follow-up meetings positive and supportive sessions. This is an opportunity to support progress that has been made, resolve issues, and clarify expectations. The first follow-up meeting should be scheduled at the end of the initial planning meeting, or at least an expectation can be stated: "Let's get together on this again after you have had your first staff training session," or "Let's meet again before Christmas vacation." The meeting times can coincide with project deadlines or the school year schedule, whichever seems appropriate.

Prior to the follow-up meeting, review your notes about the staff member or the project. Look over what you agreed on during the initial meeting and review any interim notes or jog your memory for any observations you have made since that initial planning session or since the last follow-up. One concern will be to determine what progress has been made, if the staff member is working on a specific project, and to get a picture of problems that may have arisen. Be as encouraging as possible and do not convey the impression that you are "monitoring" but that your intent is to facilitate. Give specific feedback. Tell the staff members, if appropriate, that they are doing a good job and tell them specifically what they are doing well. "You did an excellent job of organizing and conducting that last staff development workshop" is much more productive than saying, "Things seem to me to be going fine." The follow-up interview is not the time to be picky about minor details; these concerns should be made on the spot, when you observe the discrepancies or the need for change.

Make Changes as Necessary

It is important to emphasize the positive throughout the goal-setting and follow-up process; however, it is always possible that events will not occur as they were planned. Projects may fall off their initial time lines, unanticipated constraints may become apparent, and staff interest may be less than expected. Reactions to such obstacles can range from shifting the blame to uncontrollable circumstances or intransigent persons to centering the blame entirely on the individual staff member. Assessing blame is not usually an effective response; it is better to find out why the staff member has not been successful and then focus on what can be done to change the situation. Be explicit about not laying the blame on the staff member.

If things are not going as planned or as well as they might be, use the follow-up session for problem-solving activities. Even if the focus becomes the lack of accomplishment by the individual staff member, try to avoid thinking that this staff member is lazy, dumb, or irresponsible. Instead, try to find out the cause. Among the causes might be: (1) the staff member did not understand what you expected him or her to do,

(2) the staff member has had no experience or training in doing it, (3) there are no consequences if the staff member does not do it, (4) institutional or staff constraints prevent progress, and (5) there is no reward for doing it.

Each of these causes can be resolved. It is possible for you to make sure the expectations are clear and explicit. You can provide training and make sure that there are positive consequences for completion and negative consequences if the task is not completed. You may not be able to remove institutional or staff constraints, but you at least need to know that they exist so you can decide whether to pursue the issue further or not. It is important that neither the supervisor nor the staff member wallow in frustrations because the project is going slower than expected or because new roadblocks keep appearing around each corner. Blow off steam a bit, if helpful; then move on to determining what the solution might be, what the next steps are, and what the new target date is.

At the end of each follow-up meeting, you and the staff member will probably have a list of things to do. If there have been problems or delays, your list may be as long as the staff member's. Changes that you have made in the time lines with this staff member may affect other staff members or projects. You may have to rearrange your expectations of others, set new priorities, and find additional resources. You may have to visit with other staff or administrators in your effort to remove apparent roadblocks.

Follow-up sessions and interim reviews can also occur in group meetings. These sessions are more likely to be focused on the project rather than on the individual, but they can provide you with helpful information in a timely and efficient manner. Problem solving can be quite effective in small group settings in which staff view themselves as team members trying to accomplish group tasks.

Conclusion

Effective goal setting within a performance appraisal system will go a long way toward making the entire system effective. The best working environment is one in which staff goals are mutually set and the staff are provided with the support needed to achieve their goals. Research provides strong evidence that participation in setting goals can lead to higher goal accomplishment than do monetary rewards (Latham and Wexley, 1981).

References

Latham, G. P., and Wexley, K. E. *Increasing Productivity Through Performance Appraisal.* Reading, Mass.: Addison-Wesley, 1981.

Lazer, R. I., and Wikstrom, W. S. *Appraising Managerial Performance: Current Practices and Future Directions.* New York: Conference Board, 1977.

Olson, R. F. *Performance Appraisal: A Guide to Greater Productivity.* New York: Wiley, 1981.

Sanford, N. *The American College.* New York: Wiley, 1962.

An appraisal interview takes careful planning if it is going to be a useful part of the performance appraisal system.

Planning and Conducting Appraisal Interviews

Scenario: Mary is scheduled to have her annual review meeting with her boss, the director of housing. He is on the phone but motions for her to come into his office and sit down. He continues on the phone for another five or six minutes. After he hangs up, he looks through the papers on his desk and comments, "I know I had your materials here somewhere. I saw them just the other day. Oh, well, we'll just have to get along without them. Tell me how things have been going this year. Did you ever get that student assistant situation from last fall worked out?" Mary gets about three words out before the phone rings, and the director talks to the maintenance person for five minutes before hanging up and saying, "Let's see, where were we?"

Even if the performance appraisal process is viewed as a system with many facets, the end-of-the-year appraisal session remains of pivotal importance; it is the last but not least part of the system. Even an otherwise great performance appraisal system can fail because of poorly conducted annual review interviews. This chapter presents guidelines for ensuring that the review interview goes well. It looks at what you should

R. D. Brown. *Performance Appraisal as a Tool for Staff Development.*
New Directions for Student Services, no. 43. San Francisco: Jossey-Bass, Fall 1988.

do in planning the interview, describes how to conduct an interview, and presents a sample interview dialogue.

Planning the Interview

Mary's interview with her director clearly gives the impression that he was not prepared for the interview, and his behavior conveys the message that this is not an important meeting or process. The director can not find related annual review materials and perhaps has not even looked at them. He did not make arrangements to ensure that he would not be interrupted. Even if he later got around to giving full attention to the interview, lack of preparation undoubtedly would lead to discussing trivial concerns and forgetting to discuss major concerns. The staff member's reaction may range from relief that nothing negative is discussed to rage because she does not know any more about how she stands after the interview than she did before.

Many interviews between you and your staff will be impromptu; they are unplanned but focus on job performance. They may be the outcome of a crisis, a change in your unit's goals, or a casual happening. These are bound to occur. You cannot plan for these interviews. The formal appraisal interview, however, demands careful preparation. Administrators who do not prepare for an appraisal interview are neglecting their duty. The appraisal process and the interview should not be viewed as an extra, tacked-on duty but as a regular and expected part of the administrator's responsibilities. It needs to be part of all administrators' job descriptions. The following paragraphs discuss guidelines for planning the interview.

Choose an Appropriate Time and Setting. You and the staff member should be able to attend to issues at hand with minimal distractions. You should not be expecting interruptions or dealing with a distracting crisis. Avoid times when the staff member may be confronting major personal or professional problems. The timing is often dictated by deadlines for recommendations regarding salary, reappointment, and promotion. The staff member should know what the appointment is about. Announce that you would like to do your reviews during a certain period of time, and ask staff to schedule an appointment with you. Alert your secretary to the importance of these meetings so that no staff member's session is unduly delayed.

It is essential that the interview be private and that there be no unexpected interruptions. Most administrators schedule interviews in their offices, but there is no reason why they could not be held in the staff members' offices or in a neutral setting. Key elements are ensuring privacy and ensuring an environment that will put the staff member at ease.

Do not cancel a scheduled meeting unless it is absolutely necessary. When you cancel a meeting, you are saying, in effect, that something else is more important than that staff member. This is not a good message to convey, particularly if you cancel at the last minute or if the staff member is especially anxious about the meeting. Football coaches often call time out just seconds before the opponent's kicker prepares to attempt a field goal. This is supposed to make the kicker more nervous—giving him time to think about it more. You do not want to put your staff in a similar position. Most will have prepared for the session, some may have lost sleep over it, and for most it is not necessarily something they have been looking forward to. Try to make the interview process as important for you as it is for them.

Make a Fair Assessment. All appraisals involve subjective judgments; no administrator has the appraisal process reduced to a formula that requires solely the input of information from rating scales and other numerical data, which, in turn, lead to calculations and then to final judgments. Instead, the administrator must gather, consider, and weigh the information she has. These judgments must be made with care. Casual attention to the process yields minimal positive results and could easily undo the positive relationships and rapport you have established with the staff.

To make a fair and objective assessment of a staff member's performance, you need to take the steps described in the paragraphs that follow.

Gather Information. Look over the plan that was developed in planning sessions with the staff member earlier in the year. What was expected? What happened between the initial planning session and now? What has been accomplished? What events have intervened, and what circumstances have changed? You should have notes from observations you have made throughout the year. The quality or perhaps even the existence of notes on staff members is an indicator of how seriously you take the appraisal task. Administrators can easily get caught up focusing their energies on projects rather than on people, or only on people whose political influence affects them, or on inept staff who may let them down.

Now is not the time to start making your observations; they should have been made throughout the year. Even quickly jotting down notes as events occur and then filing them in one master folder or in each staff member's folder can be immensely helpful in providing feedback during an interview. Short notes to yourself, such as "John really carried the staff meeting today; just when it seemed everyone was getting discouraged, he provided several helpful and realistic suggestions" or "Mary's staff always seems to present well-organized programs; I am going to have to comment on that to her," can ensure that you do not forget key observations gleaned during the year or during the period between interviews.

Be Watchful for Bias. Rating errors were noted in Chapter Four. These same errors are possible when making your end-of-the-year judgments, and you need to be particularly watchful if you are reviewing at the same time the performance of several staff members in preparation for visiting with them individually. Because of similar interests or backgrounds, you will feel more compatible and comfortable with some staff members than with others. In fact, you may have so much to chat about that you never get around to spending quality time on appraisal feedback.

Several other biases can affect assessment during this phase. You are likely to view successful programs as due to your own work and to blame failures on the staff. Staff members, on the other hand, are likely to have the opposite view; they will blame failures on you and attribute successes to their own hard work. You have nothing to lose by generously sharing the credit with your staff, praising them individually and collectively for successful outcomes.

Administrators also tend to blame poor performance on personality characteristics. The staff member was lazy or undependable. A staff member who is habitually late with his or her reports, however, is not necessarily lazy. Perhaps there is a difference in priorities. The staff member may believe it is more important to cope with a current case of alcohol abuse in the residence hall than to write a formal report on a vandalism incident last week. Perhaps the staff member is overloaded, or his work-study help doesn't type well so he has to type reports himself. Or perhaps the staff member has inadequate time management skills. Maybe she has a writing problem and procrastinates as long as possible. Thus, chronic late reports should be viewed as a problem, and it is the task of the administrator to find out why this problem has occurred and what plan can be worked out to change the behavior, not to draw conclusions about the personality of the staff member.

Leniency biases are also possible. When a staff member whom you like or with whom you have similar interests has the same problems as another staff member with whom you don't have such rapport, you may be quicker to note extenuating circumstances or to overlook the problem in the case of your friends. Be particularly attentive to tendencies to rate staff of different genders, race, age, or nationality systematically higher or lower.

Other biases include assessing on the basis of the appearance of working hard: Sometimes the person who makes it look easy is rated lower than the person who makes it look hard. Try to be alert to overreacting to the constant complainer and constant reporter. The complainer is always at your door about something that is going wrong. As soon as you see the complainer coming, you know that you are going to have to listen to a complaint. You may rate the complainer lower because of your negative reaction to the constant barrage or higher because you don't want him back at your door again. The constant reporter is always making sure you know what the reporter is accomplishing, especially when something good happens. In contrast to persons who may feel shy about announcing their accomplishments, reporters keep you well informed about their activities. Make sure you do not undervalue the shy or modest staff members who keep their successes to themselves.

No magic cure exists to eliminate biases. As noted earlier, however, focusing on skills and abilities as exhibited in behavior, rather than on attitudes and personality, is a step in the right direction. If staff know that their accomplishments are going to be recognized, they are likely to be better motivated and more satisfied.

Remember to look at staff members' methods, as well as at their accomplishments. Did the staff members succeed but in the process alienate their own staff or students? Campus activities staff may have helped student organizations sponsor numerous highly successful events, but the process may have been one that was almost entirely managed by staff with minimal student involvement. When arriving at your final ratings, be sure to look at processes as well as outcomes.

Few people enjoy making formal judgments about others, though we make them informally all the time. Perhaps it is not the judging itself that is so painful as it is confronting the other person with our judgment. It helps to remember you are judging the work, not the person. If the appraisal process has been carefully thought through, then the process should be as fair and objective as you can make it. But there are good reasons to work extra hard to achieve that goal. A botched appraisal could damage the career of a staff member, especially if the reviews become part of a permanent record. You also risk the good faith and colleagueship of your staff in the process. Such dire possibilities are among the reasons that many supervisors feel uncomfortable about the appraisal interview and perhaps even want to avoid the task.

Consider the Appraisal Interview as an Educational Moment. If the appraisal process is viewed as an educational and developmental activity, then the interview should be viewed as an educational moment, an opportunity to recognize and reward good performance and to provide guidance when performance has not met expectations. Many professors do not like to grade papers or assign semester grades because they fail to recognize or accept appraisal as a critical part of their educational mission. For whatever reason, they have the misguided notion that assessing student progress and providing feedback and direction to students is not part of their role. To make the same mistake in performance assessment of staff is to miss an excellent opportunity to influence significantly the professional competence and perhaps the future careers of staff members. The questions you need to have in mind when making assessments and planning the interview are: "How can I help this person become a better staff member?" "Can I help a poor performer find out why he is not succeeding?" "Can I help the superior performer continue to grow?" If you approach the appraisal interview in this frame of mind, the whole process will be a more positive experience than it will be if your prime motivation is "How can I get through this process and generate the least amount of hostility?"

If you use a coaching perspective in your supervision, the annual review interview is a time when you and staff members can look carefully at their performance and note what has been done right and what needs to be worked on. Like a good coach, you acknowledge and reward the new accomplishments, the new skills gained, and you provide guidance on what changes can be made. Swimming coaches can make suggestions for improving basic strengths, sharpening key arm movements, and determining the kinds of workouts needed. They can model through demonstration, and they can observe performance and make specific suggestions. Most coaches enjoy this; it is what coaching is all about. Seeing people improve their swimming skills can be highly rewarding. Student affairs administrators can experience similar joys when supervising staff. They can play an integral role in the maturation of the new professionals and the revitalization of the mature staff. Appraisal interviews can be highly significant coaching moments.

Be Flexible in Your Role. You can assume a variety of roles in the appraisal process and in the interviews; these roles range from judge to listener, counselor, mentor, adviser, and coach. The role will be determined somewhat by the nature of your position, the expectations that your supervisor has for you, and your relationship with the staff member. Most people are uncomfortable with being the authoritarian judge, and in most situations this role can be avoided. It is important to be an effective listener and to be comfortable with providing advice. Your choice of a role may vary from staff member to staff member and even may vary within the interview itself. It helps to be consciously aware of the role shifting you may do.

Research results show that performance appraisal is more effective and staff are more satisfied if the administrator uses a style that promotes problem solving and that allows the staff member to participate actively (King, 1984). Make the staff members' problems your joint problems, not their problems. Solve the problem together. Do not expect the staff member to come up with a solution, nor should you provide a ready-made solution. If a residence director is having discipline problems within her hall, work out together how the problem can be analyzed and attacked. This provides an opportunity to model problem-solving behavior (such as using other resources, brainstorming, trying out solutions, and reevaluating progress) as well as to indicate your support for the staff member.

Conducting the Interview

The appraisal interview is the critical link in the performance appraisal system. The rest of the system can be nearly perfect, but the entire system can fall apart if the interview goes poorly. Staff members will remember what was said for at least a year and maybe even longer. What happens in the interview may motivate them to work harder and may influence them to be extremely satisfied with their jobs. What happens can also make them disgruntled, dissatisfied, and distraught. The appraisal interview takes on greater importance when there is only one such interview a year. Regular formal and informal interviews with staff help make the annual review session less threatening and enhance the probability that it will be more productive.

As you make final preparations for the interview, review what your objectives are. Set these objectives for the interview:

1. Learn what staff think of their performance.
2. Share your assessment of staff members' performance strengths and of areas needing improvement.
3. Praise good performance and agree on a plan for improvement.
4. Plan the next steps in the staff members' development.

How are you going to reach all the objectives? Do not force yourself to try to reach all the objectives in one interview. It will take practice before you know what interviews are going to take more than one session. If you do need more than one session, schedule the second session as soon as possible.

The interview can be organized around your objectives. Start the interview by establishing rapport and stating the objectives of the meeting. Then ask the staff member to present his or her self-appraisal. After you have listened to the staff member, share your perceptions. Finally, discuss plans for the next work period.

Establish Rapport. Even though you may not enjoy the interview process, you probably have more practice at it than your staff members, who are likely to be tense no matter how well they perceive they have done. Salary, being asked back for another year, promotion, and long-term career aspirations may hinge on the results of this interview. Even if none of these is at stake, the staff member's self-respect is probably on the table. So there is good cause for anxiety.

Building rapport does not necessarily mean you discuss the weather or the success of the college basketball team. It can mean discussing something of known mutual interest or acknowledging the staff member's nervousness. Sharing a personal anecdote about the time you tripped on the rug during your first interview can help convey to staff members that you know how they may be feeling. Remember that rapport is more than sharing one laugh; it is a building process whose structure can be added to or torn down in the future.

State Your Goals for the Interview. Tell the staff member what you plan to accomplish during the interview and indicate that, if time runs out, you will schedule another meeting as soon as possible. Ask staff members if they have any additions to the agenda and indicate that you will be asking for their input and reactions as you proceed. This conveys that, while you are in control of the interview, you want to make sure they participate. A successful interview will have the staff member talking at least half the time.

Ask the Staff Member to Give His or Her Self-Appraisals. One purpose of a performance appraisal system is to strengthen the self-appraisal skills of individual staff members. How well can each evaluate his or her own competencies, make appropriate adjustments, and take appropriate actions? Find out how the staff member believes the year went. By letting the staff member talk first, you gain a perspective on how well the staff member understands the goals of the unit and your expectations for his or her performance. You will now have a basis for formulating your response—what you want to confirm and praise and what you want to help the staff member work on in the future. Is the staff member overly confident or overly self-critical? Have the important objectives or behaviors been highlighted? Are the priorities the same as yours? Are you being told only what the staff member thinks you want to hear?

When the staff member is speaking, listen. This should be active listening, not passive listening where you are busy trying to think about what you are going to say next or whether you agree or disagree with the staff member. Try to grasp fully what the staff member is saying and what he or she is feeling about it. Check to see if your understanding is correct and indicate that you can be corrected.

Give Your Evaluation. Start with the positive and with the areas of agreement. It is important to recognize and confirm the positive. You may seem to be saving time if you get quickly to the few minor suggestions you have for improvement, but the staff member needs confirmation regarding accomplishments, especially if you want the staff member to continue doing these same activities. Positive feedback validates for the staff member that what he or she is doing is appropriate, recognized, and valued.

Next, comment on any self-criticism or negative appraisal comments that the staff member has made. If you believe the staff member is being too harsh on herself, indicate that your judgment differs and suggest specific reasons why your judgment differs. Say something like "I know we agreed earlier in the year that you would have three programs on study habits in your hall this semester, and you only had two. But neither of us anticipated the sore throat epidemic, and your 'Black Plague Night' with free movies and Kleenex was an innovative way of perking up the mood of the hall. It is important to be responsive to your environment and the student circumstances as well as to follow a plan."

Focus on Being Descriptive Rather Than Evaluative. How is it possible to conduct an evaluation interview without being evaluative?

Isn't that what this whole process is about? Yes, the process is an evaluative one, but the most important goal of the system is to improve future performance. Making declarations like "good" or "poor" about past performance is evaluative but does not necessarily promote a change in behavior. An accurate description of behavior is less likely to be misinterpreted, it can be corrected if misinterpreted, and it can be a more graphic evaluative comment than a judgmental statement. Saying to a staff member that "You are tactless and undiplomatic" is less likely to lead to a productive exchange than saying, "I notice that students reacted to your suggestions with disagreements, and some walked out of the room." Saying that "I sometimes see students waiting for twenty minutes or more outside your office when you are gone; why is this?" is better than saying, "You seem to be rather thoughtless about keeping appointments."

Avoid Promoting Defensiveness in the Staff Member. Assessing blame leads to defensive responses. You can avoid defensiveness by stating facts, taking a problem-solving stance, and focusing on future behavior. Most people are not at their creative best in problem solving when they are being defensive—that is, when they feel they must defend past behavior or protect their self-image. It is best to emphasize what can be done in the future. It is better to say, "You believe the training is going to take longer than you had planned and that disappoints you, but you think it is realistic to expect it to be completed in another month," than to say, "You misjudged the length of time the training would take."

Maintain a Written Record of Your Sessions. Summaries of major review sessions should be carefully written and then read and signed by the staff member. This combats a prevalent practice among administrators who say one thing in an interview and then write down something else; in particular, they may tend to be entirely positive in the interview but make critical comments in the written review. An administrator may believe that this gives her the best of both worlds because she does not risk ruining a good relationship with the staff member. She does no confronting, but at the same time she is able to record candid and perhaps negative comments for the record. In reality, this helps no one and places the administrator at risk when future problems arise. The staff member believes he is doing a good job and is likely to see no need to change. He will be shocked and angry if negative comments accumulate in a record that may later come to the surface. And he will begin to figure out that something must be amiss when he does not get the same raise as others.

Sample Interview

The following dialogue illustrates a constructive end-of-the-year appraisal interview between Sarah (the supervisor) and John (the staff member).

Sarah: Good morning, John. Did you and your wife enjoy the play I saw you at last week?

John: Yes, we certainly did. I did think it was a bit long, though.

S: It was long, but I have to admit the ending was a surprise. I would never have guessed that it would have that kind of ending.

J: I agree. I had read the play several years ago but even knowing the ending it was sort of a surprise. It was well acted.

S: Before I forget, John, I want to thank you for filling in on such short notice for Harry at the staff training session two weeks ago. We were in a really tight spot, and your volunteering really helped us out.

J: You're welcome.

S: John, as you know, I asked you and the rest of the staff to schedule these meetings with me so I could review each staff member's performance for the year. I would like to hear from you how everything has been going since our last discussion, share with you my perspectives, and have us mutually arrive at what the implications are for the future. Do you have anything else you want to discuss today?

J: I would like to talk to you about our plans for the new student orientation program sometime soon, though it does not have to be today.

S: Good, if we have time to do that we will. If we run out of time today either to finish the annual review or to get to the new student orientation program, I will schedule another time with you for later this week, if that is convenient for you. Now, we had a good discussion in January about the first half of the school year. How have things been going for you since then?

J: It has been a very busy second semester, but I believe we got some important things done and have laid the groundwork for future programming. We didn't get everything done we'd planned on, but I generally feel good about the year. I've learned a lot that is going to help in the future.

S: So you are satisfied with the year. Tell me about some of the things you are most satisfied with.

J: I guess there are two things that I think are major accomplishments. Getting the needs assessment procedure in place was important. Everybody on the staff was involved in one way or another so they would know how to work on it in the future. The follow-up study on campus leaders has been another major effort this year. We are not as far along on it as I would like to be, but we have a good start. My major disappointment is not getting a full-blown staff development program going. The staff does not seem to be as responsive to the concept as I think they should be.

S: Let's take each of these separately for a moment—the needs assessment, the follow-up, and the staff development program.

J: That sounds like a good idea.

(Sarah and John discuss these efforts—what went right, what is going wrong, what needs to be changed, and what needs to be done in the future. Here is their conversation about the staff development program.)

S: Tell me some more about the staff development program. You indicated earlier that this has been a disappointment to you.

J: Well, I am not sure whether it is the staff or me. I have asked for ideas at several staff meetings on good staff development topics and I get anything from no response to suggestions that they would rather have the day off or a day to catch up on their work. I did have a speaker in from one of the academic departments to talk about a new student development theory, but half the staff came late and several went to sleep during the presentation. I'm a bit at a loss right now.

S: Seems to me that the staff may be giving you a message.

J: That they don't want staff development!

S: Maybe that, but maybe something else, too. Any ideas?

J: They are very busy and don't have time for more meetings.

S: That's probably pretty accurate. Seems like it would help to come up with ways that they could see staff development helping them do the work they have to do. I'm not sure what those might be, but . . .

J: I wonder if we had something on time management or stress management—if they would be interested in those topics.

S: Those sound like excellent ideas, though you would want to be sure that these came across as ways to help improve the quality of their lives, not just ways to make them more productive. I wonder if the needs assessment process for determining student interests that you described earlier wouldn't work for your own staff. Maybe a two-person committee could be in charge and gather staff ideas.

J: That's a good idea. I'll check with a couple of staff and see what they think. Maybe if they put together their own staff development program, it would be better received and more meaningful and useful.

(They discuss briefly who these two staff members might be and how the needs assessment might follow the model of the student needs assessment program recently worked out. Sarah asks for feedback later on how this works out; if appropriate, John might wish to share the idea with other directors at a directors' staff meeting.)

S: John, as you know, each year I put together a summary report on each director that covers the following areas of the job: management, staff supervision, working with students and other staff, and responsibility and commitment. I gave you this list earlier and asked you to be thinking about each of these. What we have talked about thus far fits into several of those categories. Let's discuss each one, starting with management. This includes planning and organizing and handling the daily operational decisions. Why don't you give me some examples that indicate how you have done in this area? Then I will comment and share feedback I have from your ratings gathered from other directors and your own staff.

(John and Sarah go over each of the categories. John gives himself a rating and provides examples of things he has done or achieved that support the rating. Sarah shares ratings and examples compiled from observations that she has made and from other input. They then close with the following dialogue.)

S: I want to say again how good I feel about you being one of our directors. You have made significant progress during your first two years with us, and I am sure that you will continue to grow. Your contributions have meant a lot to our total effectiveness and to how we are viewed by others on campus.

J: Thanks.

S: I will be writing a summary of our discussion and getting a copy to you shortly. I would like you to look it over carefully as our annual review procedure suggests. Let me know of any corrections. Also, I will need you to sign a final copy. I look forward to seeing you next week to talk some more about the new student orientation program, and at that time we can set up a session to see how the staff development effort is going.

This sample interview can be used as a role-playing exercise during a staff development training session, or it could be used as the basis for a discussion at a directors' meeting. Another use is to stimulate staff and directors to create their own vignettes.

Conclusion

An interview is more impromptu than a planned speech, but it demands an equal amount of preparation. Consider the homework you do prior to a job interview on an unfamiliar campus. Your preparation for interviewing one of your staff members should involve a comparable level of study and concentration. When conducting the interview, keep in mind the purpose: the improvement of the staff member's quality of work life and job performance. A good behavioral check on the quality of the interview is the ratio of talking that you do compared to that of the staff member. Rarely will a good interview be one in which you do most of the talking. These two rules, keeping the purpose in mind and keeping your talk ratio low, will go a long way toward making the interview a successful one.

Reference

King, P. *Performance Planning and Appraisal: A How-To Book for Managers.* New York: McGraw-Hill, 1984.

*Problems can arise when dealing with poor performers,
super performers, and legal considerations.*

Problem Situations
in Performance Appraisal

Scenario: Conversation between Peter (director of campus
activities) and Mary (vice-president for student affairs).

Peter: I just read an excellent sourcebook on performance
appraisal systems for student affairs. I wonder if we should
be looking at designing a system for us?

Mary: We already have a system. We have a rating form
that we have been using for ten years and an annual review
process that I haven't heard any complaints about.

P: Maybe we can improve the system we now have. Besides,
it might be a good idea to get more people involved in
working with it. We have a lot of new directors, and I
remember when I came on board I had no idea how to
evaluate staff performance.

M: I don't think you really need to worry about a system
for most staff; they are going to do their job anyway. And
the so-called system never works for problem situations anyway. But let's bring it up at the next directors' meeting and
see what reaction we get.

R. D. Brown. *Performance Appraisal as a Tool for Staff Development.*
New Directions for Student Services, no. 43. San Francisco: Jossey-Bass, Fall 1988.

Even the best planning with the best performance appraisal system will not prevent problems. Staff may react in unpredictable ways, your supervisor may react in unpredictable ways, and perhaps even you might react in unpredictable ways in different situations. No system can anticipate all the possible variations that might occur. Even if the system does a reasonable job, some appraisal situations are more difficult to deal with than others, and each student affairs administrator needs to recognize this.

This chapter looks at ways to discover the source of problems, illustrates how problems with poor and super performers might be handled, and examines some of the legal issues in performance appraisal.

Finding the Source of the Problems

It is highly unlikely that a superb performance appraisal system will exist within a student affairs unit that is otherwise poorly managed. Problems within a system, however, are likely to be indicators of other management problems. If there are problems with the appraisal system, first look at the system itself for what might be wrong, then look at the entire management system, and finally look at individual supervisors.

Within the performance appraisal system, there could be several sources of problems. The system may require too much paperwork, or it may be too involved and have too many steps. The costs of any system must be balanced by the benefits. Costs include staff time and energy as well as expenses for printing forms and other materials. Benefits include increased efficiency, productivity, satisfaction, and morale. If a system has a negative impact (for example, if it lowers job satisfaction and staff morale), then not only will the benefits be lower but there will also be higher costs (including job searches to replace disgruntled staff). Perhaps the system is too complex, or the staff has not had sufficient training to make the system work. More often than not, the problems are less likely to be with the system itself than with how the system is implemented.

Maybe the structure and overall management style of the unit are incongruent with the appraisal system. There could be an imbalance between the formality or informality of the performance appraisal system and how the student affairs unit is structured and managed. A highly informal unit may find a highly structured performance appraisal system a poor fit. A staff that is accustomed to highly structured decision making may find mutual goal setting, self-evaluations, and peer appraisals uncomfortable tasks. Any vagueness about who is to do what and who reports to whom is going to become apparent as you try to establish a performance appraisal system. If unit goals are unclear, it is going to be difficult to integrate individual staff member goals or subunit goals with the goals of the overall student affairs office.

It is essential that supervisors have the respect, trust, and confidence of their staff. If staff members fear for their jobs, any performance appraisal system will be threatening and not conducive to high performance or to a good working climate. A supervisor may not have expertise in all facets of the unit being supervised, and this needs to be acknowledged and dealt with. A chief student affairs officer may not know the inner workings and responsibilities of all student affairs subunits, such as financial aid or housing. A new director in any unit may not know the detailed responsibilities within her own unit and may be unsure about interrelationships with other units. In such situations, however, it is possible to deal with the issue of lack of detailed knowledge by admitting it and by gaining the support of staff, while, at the same time, you note that you have expertise in other important areas. Do not expect to obtain credibility with your staff, however, unless you demonstrate an authentic interest in their roles and responsibilities and in their expectations of you.

If the source of the problems lies outside of the performance appraisal system, do not expect the problems to be solved by forcing the appraisal system to fit. If the unit goals are unclear or if staff responsibilities and reporting lines are not delineated, the appraisal process is going to be muddled. You and the staff need to resolve these issues before trying to design and implement a performance appraisal system.

Dealing with Problem Cases

Once you have sorted out what problems relate to the appraisal system and what problems of the unit management interact with the appraisal system, you have a good idea of where to focus your problem-solving priorities. Your troubles do not stop there, however. As Mary noted in the opening vignette, there are problem cases that do not always fit the expected pattern. These exceptions can easily taint your feelings about the appraisal process, and they may have a detrimental impact on the entire system. Three problems cases are likely to give you the most trouble: (1) the poor or disgruntled staff member, (2) the super performer, and (3) cases that raise legal issues.

Appraising the Poor or Disgruntled Staff Member. If administrators tend to avoid performance appraisals, they tend to avoid appraising staff members in particular. This is understandable. It is much easier to praise and reward (although not enough praising and rewarding are done) an excellent staff member than it is to confront a staff member who has not fulfilled your expectations. How do you work with a staff member who has not been doing well? Here are several questions you need to ask; suggested actions, depending on your answers, follows.

Is the staff member's performance inadequate? You have evidence that a staff member has not been performing well. Reports have been late, other staff rate the person's performance low, and you have several complaints from students. You recall that the staff member seldom contributes to discussions at staff meetings. At this point, there is no single glaring incident or failure that stands out. What should you do?

You need to sort out carefully perceptions and conclusions based on work performance of the staff member from those based on his or her attitudes and personality. If, as I have noted in the earlier chapters, you have used appraisal measures that assess behaviors, it will be easier to make these distinctions. But it is important to double-check your perceptions when you are making these judgments and preparing to take action.

Another check to make is to ascertain that the poor performance is due to factors within the control of the staff member and not due to circumstances within the setting. Has the staff member had enough support? Have there been unusual circumstances that affect his or her performance? Have other staff members had similar problems but coped with them?

Do not let the double-checking of your assessment be another excuse to procrastinate and avoid confronting the staff member. This risks allowing problems to escalate, and soon you may be facing a dismissal situation rather than helping a staff member over some temporary rough spots. Give staff members the benefit of the doubt, and always be ready and open to accept evidence that differs from the opinion you are forming about their performance. Eventually, however, you must act on the evidence that is available to you and make the best judgment you can.

How does the staff member react to criticism? You do not like to criticize, and your staff do not like to receive criticism. It is natural for most staff to react defensively to criticism. These reactions may take several forms. The staff member may deny that a problem even exists. She didn't know anything went wrong, or he didn't think it was "such a big deal." Another response is to blame someone else. The poor performer may blame another staff member, students for not being mature, administrative red tape, or even you for not providing clear instructions or support. It is important to let the staff member talk. Staff in such situations need time to think through their reaction to the criticism and to determine your level of seriousness.

Some staff will hear the criticism, verbally agree with the criticism, but not make any changes in their behavior. This may be because they want to get on to other issues, because they really don't agree but do not wish to make an issue of their disagreement, or because they do not really understand the nature of the criticism. It is important to determine whether their verbal acceptance is real or not. You can determine this by acknowledging the agreement and then working toward a resolution that will lead to behavioral changes. Try to determine the cause for the criticized behavior, and see if this suggests what changes in future behavior are necessary. The focus must remain on future behavior rather than on past faults. If a director has not been providing enough direct supervision for his or her own staff, what specific actions will be taken to change this pattern? If a staff member has been repeatedly late for meetings with students, what time management adjustments are going to be made to ensure promptness? If a division coordinator continually underestimates budgets for projects, what support can he or she solicit from another staff member who can assist in the future?

Occasionally, a staff member may become so upset by the situation that he announces, "I quit." If there has been enough tension and acrimony, you may be tempted to respond with, "OK." This is a mistake, though at the time it may seem an easy way out of a difficult and uncomfortable situation. The staff member should be given sufficient time to reconsider his or her position, and you may want time to reconsider yours. Do you really want the staff member to leave? Does this seem to be an irresolvable situation? You may both decide that resignation is the best choice, but do not let that be decided during emotional stress.

Is the staff member trying to improve? Assuming that you are comfortable with the accuracy of your evidence that the staff member is not performing as expected, an important appraisal question remains: Is the staff member working to improve his performance? Did he really understand what was expected? Does she have the training and skills necessary to do the job? Were the expectations realistic? Your answers to these questions will help shape how you and the staff member will work through the situation. If the staff member is trying to do the job well, you need to make a determination as to whether or not he needs more training, closer supervision, or a transfer to another position.

If the staff member is working hard to improve, this is probably someone with whom you will wish to spend more time, for whom you may make adjustments in the job expectations, or for whom you will wish to search for another appropriate position if she or he does not fit the current position.

Emphasize the person's strengths and build on these. You must be careful, however, if you redesign a position for one staff member, particularly if this means a work-load reduction. Other staff members in comparable positions may resent being expected to do more work or more distasteful work if another staff member is relieved of similar responsibilities.

What if the staff member is not trying hard to get the job done or to improve? Assuming that you have progressed through the other processes of planning, observing, and seeking his or her opinions and input, and you still find no changes or no apparent motivation to change, what do you do? You can probably think of such situations that are before you right now. For example, a staff member does not agree with the goals that were set or how and when he was to accomplish them. This situation suggests that he doesn't see either enough reward or enough negative consequences to warrant changing his behavior. You may be trying to shift the emphasis in your unit to more outreach and developmental activities whereas the staff member finds it easy enough to fill his schedule with day-to-day problem student cases. The staff member sees no benefits to a change of behavior.

This can happen among senior staff as often or more than it does among younger staff. It can be someone who believes she or he should have been hired for your position, someone who has been on the same campus longer than you have been, someone who used to report to your supervisor but must now report to you, or someone who appears, on the surface at least, just to be waiting for retirement. These are not uncommon situations, and often the response is to try to work around the person or patiently wait for his or her retirement. This is not a good solution. What else can be done?

For change to occur, particularly with disgruntled staff, the staff member has to see that there are benefits to changing his or her behavior and that there are consequences to not changing. Kid-glove treatment may be the preferred approach, and certainly the feelings of the persons involved need to be considered. But this may not work. How can you reward the person for cooperating? Can you offer alternative job assignments, additional help with difficult or disagreeable assignments, or other incentives? You have probably already appealed to the individual's loyalty; now you must offer tangible rewards, but they do not have to be monetary nor do they have to be bribes. What are possible negative consequences short of termination? Consider your options: minimal salary increase, demotion, transfer to a less preferred position? Easy solutions are not often readily available, and that is why it is easy to procrastinate.

Terminating a Staff Member. Termination may be best for the staff member in the long run, but that is not sufficient to mask the uncomfortableness you feel when you have to fire someone. You have a multitude of feelings about the situation: You feel sorry for the staff member you must fire. You worry about how they are going to react. You know their good side and maybe know something about their personal life and wonder how they will cope. You may question your judgment in hiring them in the first place or feel anger at the person who previously held your position and who may have let the situation get out of control, leaving you with few options. How will this affect the other staff? Have they taken sides? Will it make them fearful, more motivated, or resentful? Questions and feelings like these are bound to arise, and most administrators will have them regardless of their experience and apparent capacity to bite the bullet. In a college or university setting, semester breaks and the end of the school year are natural periods for making rehiring or termination decisions. This encourages procrastination in dealing with difficult and problem staff members; you may hope they will make the decision to leave on their own.

It is particularly important to maintain your documentation efforts in a case that results in termination, especially when the situation involves a member of one of the protected classes. With a good appraisal system, you should have at your fingertips all the needed information and have in place all the needed processes that are fair and legal. On the assumption, however, that your system is less than perfect, when dealing with the possible termination of a member of a protected class, make sure your records are complete and that you are following the appropriate procedures.

Termination should be the last resort and not used as a threat; you should have minimal guilt feelings because you have gone the limit. Three keys to a relatively clean termination include: (1) documentation, (2) existence of a process, and (3) making it an educational moment.

Poor performance is probably the most frequent cause for termination, but other reasons sometimes become the rationale for the action. Gross violations of policies (such as providing alcohol to legal minors) are probably more readily documented than is not doing the job as expected—that is, unless you have followed the suggestions noted earlier, have had a clear, well-defined set of job-related behaviors, and have had appropriately documented planning and review sessions. Gathering documentation once you have decided to fire someone is necessary but can be insufficient if you have no prior record of your expectations, agreements, and the person's performance.

The process of termination should include a clear verbal warning, a final written warning, and then written termination. The staff member should be told that her job is in jeopardy and the reasons given. This should be clearly stated so there is no doubt in her mind about your seriousness. Indicate specifically what behaviors she will have to change to retain her position. These should be observable behaviors or actions she must take. Provide a realistic time line for her to provide evidence of change. Write a record of what was said and what were your expectations. This could be sent to the staff member. Doing so provides you with a double-check of whether or not the staff member understood the specifics and the seriousness of the situation and your expectations. You undoubtedly still hope that the staff member will measure up to your expectations this time or that she will decide to leave of her own accord.

If no improvement is noted after this process, the next step is a final notice. Again, you write a memo, call the staff member in, and specify exactly what behavior must be changed and within what time line. The time period should be relatively short. This is the time, if not earlier, to notify your own supervisor of the steps you are taking. It is helpful to have an appeal process built into the system, and, when final notice is given, the staff member should be given the necessary information about filing an appeal if he or she wishes to do so.

Even if the termination process goes the full route, educational moments are still possible, and you can make final termination less painful for all concerned. Remember that, although you cannot directly control the staff member's behavior, you do have control over what you say and do. You must hold firm, but you need not be brutal. Allow the staff member room to maintain his self-respect. Emphasize his strengths and allow him to be defensive, if necessary. This is an emotional moment for the staff member, so do not expect rationality to prevail—rationalization, yes. You may wish to share with the staff member what kind of letter of reference you would write, if asked. Again, it is important for you to keep notes on what was said at this last meeting and to file this with the staff member's records.

Quite likely, this is not the last you will hear of the staff member. In a month or maybe in five years, you may get a phone call requesting a letter of reference from the staff member or from someone considering hiring the staff member. No easy solution exists as to how to handle these requests except to suggest caution. Because of the litigious nature of society today, many in the same situation either say nothing or say nothing but good words about the staff member. Most letters of reference these days are so glowing that the person being recommended seems more like a candidate for canonization or the Nobel Prize than for a counseling center or residence hall staff position. Because of this, even the slightest hint of a negative statement often puts the job candidate at the bottom of the hiring list.

As a result, some student affairs professionals bounce from job to job, institution to institution, leaving a checkered history behind them with each new employer not knowing the full nature of the problems left behind. This has its benefits for the staff member, who now can turn over a new leaf. However, it also often perpetrates the pattern of behavior, and the staff member may eventually be in a position to cause harm because no previous employer was willing to fire the person.

Several options are open to you when asked for a reference for a terminated staff member. You can refuse to comment. You can write a bland letter mentioning only the person's good qualities, or you can write a letter with indirect references to problem areas in the person's performance. You can also recommend that interested persons contact you by phone.

If in doubt, it is probably best to be cautious. You do not want your institution faced with a lawsuit if you can help it, and you do believe that people can change, so why not give the person the benefit of the doubt? This does not mean you should lie; your own credibility and judgment are at stake as well as the new position for a former staff member when you are writing a letter of reference. Be as descriptive as you can in your letters, and make these descriptions of behaviors, not attitudes or personality. This is a good suggestion for all letters of reference, whether you are describing a staff member who was superb in her position or one whom you were happy to see leave. Behavioral descriptions of the poor performer permit readers to make their own judgment, and similar descriptions of the top performers provide readers with an understanding of the top-notch worker and what to expect from that person as compared to other applicants. The best advice is to be sure that you are not being influenced by personal animosity, that you are being factually accurate, and that your comments are job related. Also make sure that you cite personal experiences or include documentation (Vander Waerdt, 1987).

Finally, do not sweep the termination under the institutional rug. You may well not wish to make public to the rest of the staff the reasons for the termination. But two educational opportunities present themselves whenever there is a termination. You can use the opportunity to share with the staff the process that was used. This should be relatively easy to do without referring to specific behaviors. You can explain the warnings, the efforts to determine cause and to provide support, and the general circumstances of the final decision. Also, you can use this as a problem-solving task for involved staff. What are the implications for the replacement? Are there insights and suggestions on how this can be prevented in the future? Maybe staff will now see that there were earlier signs of problems that they failed to recognize or failed to respond to at the appropriate time. The goal is not to assess blame for past negligence but to prevent similar problems in the future.

Appraising the Superstar Performer. Every staff is blessed with individuals who continually fulfill all expectations and more. These professionals are self-starters, innovative, conscientious, need minimal supervision, and are excellent role models for other staff. Why worry about them? Well, you may not need to worry about them, but you do need to spend time thinking about them, talking to them, working to maintain and improve their level of satisfaction, and creating opportunities for them to continue to learn and grow. You must manage your time and priorities so that you do not neglect the needs of these staff superstars just because you are constantly dealing with crises brought to you from the poor performers. Your star performers have their own ups and downs and their own perceived failures as well as successes. They need feedback when they are doing a good job and assurances that they are valued.

Assuming that you do the best you can within your salary guidelines to reward your star performers financially, what else can you do to make them feel appreciated? First, be free with your compliments. Make them specific, direct to the person, do it often, and try to be the first one (King, 1984). Second, make other rewards available, such as sending the person to a national convention, allowing him to share the podium with you at a presentation, or providing her with needed equipment or help. Third, ask staff members why they work hard, and make sure your rewards are consistent with their needs. Find out what would make their professional life more rewarding. Finally, encourage the staff member to add to her repertoire of skills, abilities, and experiences rather than only do more of the same. Support growth by encouraging staff to learn more, not necessarily to do more.

Superstars are typically not seen as problem cases—at least not until they leave because they feel neglected. This brief examination of this concern is intended to encourage you to make a conscious effort to work with the superstars as well as with the poor performers. When you make a calendar note to yourself to work on the problem of a poor performer, balance this with a reminder to spend some time with one of your super performers.

Looking at Legal Concerns

Performance appraisal systems are used to make decisions about promotions; thus, they are considered a test and are subject to the Equal Employment Opportunity Commission (EEOC) guidelines. Although performance appraisal systems may not have to meet the rigid requirements held for personnel examinations, the courts expect such systems to be fair and accurate. The law requires that performance appraisals: (1) use job-related and valid criteria (not personality characteristics), (2) use forms and scales derived from a job analysis, (3) not be biased against any person because of race, color, sex, religion, age, or nationality, and (4) be performed by persons who have knowledge of the person and the job (King, 1984).

The validity question is the critical one. Do the criteria and the manner in which performance is assessed reflect actual job performance requirements? Does the system assess how well the staff perform their job tasks and not how well they are liked by their colleagues, or is it susceptible to biases because of different political or religious beliefs? Chapter Eight provides a description of how validity can be determined.

If the procedures described in this sourcebook are followed (a job analysis is done, a behavioral job description is prepared, behaviorally anchored rating forms are used, administrative staff are trained, and staff are involved in planning and implementation), then the evolving system should be valid and legal (Alpander, 1982). If in doubt, check with your local campus legal adviser or the affirmative action office.

At first, these potential problems may make creating an appraisal system seem tantamount to opening a Pandora's box. You did not know what you were getting into before you started developing a more formal appraisal system. Ignorance seemed like bliss. Why not save yourself time and much effort by discarding any semblance of an appraisal system and relying instead on intuition, word of mouth, and tradition? If this is your decision, you may be lucky, and problems may never surface. Efficiency and staff morale may gradually erode, but you may think you can recoup these when time permits. Even if this works, however, you will be flirting with legal disaster.

Maintaining a legal performance appraisal system demands vigilance in noting changes in official regulations and interpretations as well as day-to-day attention to the system's operation. You and others making staffing decisions need to:

- Record all staffing decisions
- Have specific, written job requirements
- Share your appraisals only with the staff member and others who need to know
- Let the staff member see the appraisal report and provide an avenue for appeal
- Never say anything in a reference that you cannot support with specific documentation
- Avoid letting personal characteristics of staff members influence your appraisals.

Making Promotion and Salary Decisions

It is undoubtedly clear that the focus of this sourcebook has been on performance appraisal as a tool for staff development rather than for salary or promotion decisions. Nevertheless, throughout the volume, the relative merits of different approaches as they relate to salary or promotion considerations have been described. I have noted, for example, that discussions with staff about promotion and salary issues should be separate from mentoring or coaching sessions. Ranking was noted as a helpful strategy for making salary determinations, but it was also noted that ranking did not by itself provide an accurate index of the distance between staff members in the quality of their performance. A staff member may be ranked fifth, but there may be so small a difference in quality of performance from the number one person that even a slight change on one performance indicator would dramatically change the rank. Using colleague appraisals or self-evaluation information for salary determinations would be questionable without additional supportive data. Using goal accomplishment as a criterion for making salary decisions can be useful, but you have to be sure that goal expectations from staff member to staff member were relatively equal or that you can arrive at a system that weights the goals equitably.

Unfortunately, most administrators are not in a position to promise salary increases at the beginning of the year based on what the staff member accomplishes during the year. Budgets are never that predictable. Events that affect performance are never that easily defined. Some administrators like to keep all salary determinations a mystery because this supposedly adds to their power. Consistent with the openness of the appraisal process espoused in this sourcebook, I recommend that at least the process for determining salaries and the criteria affecting these decisions be as open as possible.

Conclusion

It is not possible to elaborate on all the potential problem cases that can arise. A good system that has evolved through the steps outlined in Chapters One through Six will not prevent all the possible headaches, but it should prevent major catastrophes. More important, a good performance appraisal system will use even the problem cases as educational moments for you, for the particular staff member involved, and for the rest of your staff.

References

Alpander, G. G. *Human Resources Management Planning.* New York: AMACOM, 1982.

King, P. *Performance Planning and Appraisal: A How-To Book for Managers.* New York: McGraw-Hill, 1984.

Vander Waerdt, L. "How to Maintain Your Integrity and Avoid Liability for Giving Honest References." *Chronicle of Higher Education,* October 7, 1987, pp. B2-3.

Usefulness, accuracy, and credibility are the most critical
criteria for a successful performance appraisal system.

Evaluating a Performance Appraisal System

Scenario: Conversation between John (campus activities
director) and Mary (director of financial aid).

John: Mary, I've read about the procedures for staff performance appraisal, and I would like to talk to you about them.
Mary: Sure, John, what would you like to know?
J: This procedures manual that was given to me when I
started the job this year has an excellent description of
what appears to be a good performance appraisal process.
But I cannot find any of the forms or reports in the files
left by my predecessor, and the secretary doesn't remember
seeing any.
M: That isn't surprising. I don't think your predecessor
used any forms. He really didn't believe in any formal
performance appraisal process.
J: But this manual makes it sound like this process is
required of everybody. The manual was included as part of
the accreditation materials last year. That's where I got a
copy. Doesn't anybody use it? How about you?
M: I do the interviews—the usual end-of-the-year reviews—
but not much more. We spent a lot of time designing the

R. D. Brown. *Performance Appraisal as a Tool for Staff Development.*
New Directions for Student Services, no. 43. San Francisco: Jossey-Bass, Fall 1988.

system described in the manual, but we never really got
around to implementing it, and I am certainly not going to
be the one to take the first step.

J: That seems like a shame.

M: Maybe. We started to implement it, but problems kept
arising, and I think everybody just gave up.

More systems have been designed on paper than will ever be
known, and many have been abandoned for lack of care. New cars need
less upkeep, such as oil changes, than older models, but performance
appraisal systems need constant attention to keep the minor squeaks
from becoming major problems. They require patience if any semblance
of perfection is expected, and tolerance of weaknesses if they are to be
implemented with grace.

Performance appraisal systems are like the people they are
intended to evaluate. They become stagnant if not nurtured. The system
needs to be monitored and evaluated, and every effort must be made
continually to improve it.

Two questions provide a focus for evaluating a performance
appraisal system: (1) Is it being implemented as intended, and (2) is the
system accurate and dependable? Let us look closely at each of these.

Is the System Being Implemented as Intended?

As in this chapter's opening scenario, systems for appraising staff
can look good on paper but be found lacking when implemented. Here
are several questions to ask yourself about the implementation of your
performance appraisal system:

*Are middle-management directors rewarded for performance appraisal
activities?* No performance appraisal system will be effective if it is not
supported at the highest level, and this support must take the form of
rewarding middle-management staff for implementing and using an
appraisal system. You can give lip service to these activities and provide
modest support with a half-day workshop during the school year, but it
takes a greater commitment for a housing director, counseling center director, or campus activities director to spend time with individual staff, providing them with feedback during the year and serving as a resource
person or perhaps even as a mentor to junior staff members. These directors are more likely to devote time to appraising their staff if they believe
this activity is valued by those who supervise them. Does their job description and the expectations their supervisors have for them include staff
performance appraisal? How does the chief student affairs officer evaluate
the performance of her middle managers? Is performance appraisal part
of the criteria?

Is a performance appraisal system seen as an integral part of staff development? The two need to be closely related. Each unit director should know that there are expectations for staff development based on staff appraisals. A good appraisal system will help make decisions about salary and promotion easier, but a good system will also help staff and management make decisions about how performance can be improved—how they can become better advisers, better consultants, better counselors, and better supervisors.

It is important that staff development be listed as one criterion for evaluating performance of middle managers throughout student affairs. It is equally important that excellence in this performance domain be recognized and rewarded.

Do management staff receive training and assistance in performance appraisal? As noted earlier, the best-designed appraisal system can easily go awry if it is improperly implemented and used. No system is perfect, but also no system is better than the skill level of those who implement it.

Do not be misled by the relative simplicity of an appraisal system, by the small number of staff being appraised, or by the fact that the management staff are apparently caring persons or have advanced degrees. It is just as important for appraisal to be done well with one staff member as it is with many—maybe more important because that one person is probably essential to the operation of the entire unit and, whether she stays, leaves, or botches her job, her actions could have a severe negative impact. Few people you hire will have had much training in performance appraisal regardless of their educational level or level of experience. They will not know your system or expectations. Expect new staff to receive training and returning staff to sharpen their skills.

As noted in Chapter Four, training should include how to use assessment tools such as rating forms and how to conduct appraisal interviews. Most student affairs staff members and middle managers have good interpersonal skills, but the appraisal interview process is distinct enough from the usual counseling or coaching interview to warrant special training and practice.

Are job descriptions and goal-setting activities focused on behavioral and job-related activities and standards? The need for a behavioral approach has been stressed throughout this volume. Descriptors of job activities and standards for assessing performance must be as behavioral as possible. Ratings on such traits as industriousness, resourcefulness, and creativity are unacceptable under the uniform selection guidelines (Civil Service Commission, Equal Employment Opportunity Commission, Department of Justice, and Department of Labor, 1977).

Behavioral goals are not advantageous because they are easier to assess and because they make judgments about staff easier but because they communicate clearly what is expected. Research indicates that the goal to "do your best" does not result in as high performance as does having well-defined and measurable goals (Olson, 1981). Knowing specifically what is expected provides the staff member and the evaluator with clear guidelines for behavior, provides indicators for feedback, and can facilitate staff development.

Are staff involved in designing and updating the appraisal system? Staff will be directly affected by the presence or absence of an effective and fair appraisal system. Their participation is vital. Staff should be extensively involved in helping to evaluate the system as well as in designing it. If middle managers are held accountable for conducting appropriate performance appraisals and tying them to staff development efforts, staff will be a major source of information about how often appraisal activities occur and what their impact is. A good appraisal system should help staff members answer these questions about themselves (Olson, 1981): What is expected of me? How am I doing? Where am I going? How can I improve?

Do the appraisal interviews occur as intended? You probably have sent off and completed numerous performance appraisal rating forms. But how many times have you received a questionnaire that asked you how your appraisal interview went? This is a highly neglected dimension of evaluating a performance appraisal system. The appraisal interview remains a mysterious process. It is essential that any follow-up survey of the appraisal interview process be kept confidential, preferably anonymous. There should be no way to identify the respondents. Once you have worked out a procedure that guarantees anonymity, there is some helpful information you can garner.

Here is some of the information that you could collect: (1) amount of warning notice about the interview, (2) how much time the staff member spent in preparing for the interview, (3) how long the interview lasted, (4) how fair the staff member thought the appraisal was, (5) how the staff member felt after the interview (for example, motivated to improve, discouraged, angry, pleased with self), and (6) what the staff member's perceptions were of the interviewer's behavior (such as who did the talking and how were disagreements handled).

A similar form could be given to the interviewers for their global responses to all their interviews. The interviewers' self-ratings could be compared to the average ratings of those they interviewed. This process could be initiated by the interviewers themselves. Perhaps a committee of middle-management staff could arrive at a consensus form for the interviewee and themselves. This would be an excellent technique for showing concern for self-improvement through the appraisal system.

Is the System Accurate and Dependable?

Among the standards available for evaluating appraisal systems, the most promising are those being developed by the Joint Committee on Standards for Educational Evaluation (Stufflebeam and Brethower, 1987). The standards focus on four major criteria: utility (are the evaluations informative, timely, and useful?), feasibility (are the evaluations practical, politically viable, and adequately supported?), propriety (are the evaluations legal, ethical, and do they consider the welfare of those being evaluated?), and accuracy (are the evaluations valid and reliable?). These criteria can serve as the framework for your own evaluations of and improvements to your performance appraisal system.

Utility. The utility standards are critical. Does the system provide administrators with information useful for making decisions about salary and promotions, identifying training needs, helping staff improve their performance, and providing documentation for legal purposes? Perhaps no system should be expected to provide information equally well for all these purposes; perhaps it does not need to. What priorities do you or your staff have for the performance appraisal system?

Usefulness is also affected by the timeliness of the information and the power or influence that the appraisal information has. Collecting information or conducting interviews after the related decisions have been made is obviously inappropriate but unfortunately is not as rare as it should be. Credibility is important. If important decision makers do not find the information believable, then the system has little value.

Usefulness is determined as much by practical considerations as by the psychometric characteristics of the tools. You hope, of course, that the system will help you make decisions about the staff: Does the system help you decide whom to hire, retain, and promote, or how to provide specific guidance or suggestions for training? But the system can also be useful in other ways. It does not have to influence you to make a decision you would not have made without it. If it does no more than confirm or make you more confident about the decisions you must make, then the system is serving a useful purpose. It may also be useful because it provides accountability for you to your staff and because it serves staff members as a motivator or morale builder and provides them with helpful feedback for self-improvement.

Feasibility. Feasibility standards require that appraisal systems be easy to implement, be efficient, and be adequately supported. A good performance appraisal system will maintain a delicate balance between being thorough, detailed, and comprehensive but not being too cumbersome, time consuming, and costly. Implementation is going to take time and effort, but, if viewed as compatible with unit goals and integrated with staff development efforts, an efficient system will be accepted and used. If, however, the tasks become onerous for administrators and staff alike because of excessive paperwork and red tape, then the system will quickly unravel.

Is the system supported by the chief student affairs officer, and is it accepted by middle-management staff and other staff? Does top management work to implement and improve the system, to train staff, and do they model appropriate performance appraisal procedures themselves? Indicators of management acceptance include reports and other evidence that managers have spent time defining realistic goals for staff, that they conduct regular appraisal review sessions, expect high performance from themselves and others, indicate they have learned from the appraisal process, and provide mechanisms for staff to react and influence the appraisal process (Olson, 1981). Do staff find the feedback they receive helpful and accurate?

Propriety. Propriety standards demand that appraisals be legal, ethical, and conducted with appropriate regard for the welfare of the persons being appraised. Comments made in Chapter Seven about legal issues apply to these standards as do comments throughout this volume about tying performance appraisal to staff development. Ultimately the goal of any performance appraisal system should be to provide better services and educational programs for students. The entire educational community should benefit: management, those being appraised, and students.

As much as you might wish to keep the process informal and not get bogged down by legal issues, it is important nevertheless to have written guidelines. These guidelines should specify who does what, when, and for what purpose. The nature of records, feedback, and appeal processes should be spelled out.

Accuracy. Accuracy is the final, but not the least important, standard. A performance appraisal system must be able to stand the scrutiny demanded by these questions: (1) Is the system accurate? Does the information obtained accurately reflect staff performance? (2) Is the system consistent? Are the ratings a supervisor gives a staff member today consistent with the ratings that same supervisor gave last week or would give next week? These questions focus on what psychometrists refer to as validity and reliability. Usually, the concepts of validity and reliability are thought to apply primarily to paper and pencil tests or rating forms, but they are applicable and equally important concepts for any assessment activity, whether it involves a test, a rating scale, or an observation. And they apply to an entire appraisal system as well as to an individual form or scale. A rating form can be highly valid and reliable, for example, but, because it is used inappropriately, the entire appraisal system may be invalid and unreliable.

Because of the technical nature of these criteria, this chapter provides an in-depth look at validity and reliability concepts as they apply to performance appraisal efforts in student affairs.

Validity. Validity is the most important criterion for an assessment tool or evaluation procedure. An expert mechanic can examine your car, and, on the basis of the report, you may contract for expensive repairs. However, if the mechanic's diagnostic assessment is inaccurate, your car still may not get you to the next town without breaking down. You may use a comprehensive and extensive appraisal form to rate the performance of residence hall health aides, but it may be no better than asking the aides to rate themselves if the results of the form do not accurately reflect their performance.

Several forms of validity exist; one of the most important for performance appraisal is content validity: Does the tool or process accurately assess job performance? To determine whether or not the process has content validity, you must answer several questions. First, is any aspect of the job performance omitted? Is there an important task expected of the residence hall director, such as supervision of staff, that is not being assessed? Is working with faculty in program planning an important dimension of the dean of students' position, and is it covered in the assessment procedure? Second, are there behaviors being assessed that are not job related? Are you gathering information, for example, on the staff member's ability to delegate authority when the person has no one reporting to him?

Finally, are the job performance dimensions appropriately represented in the data collected? It is possible to have all dimensions represented but to have them inappropriately weighted because there are more questions about one job task than another. Suppose you find that the rating form used to assess the performance of residence hall directors contains questions of which 90 percent focus on how well a residence hall director manages the maintenance needs and discipline procedures in the hall and only 10 percent concern counseling and educational roles. If the philosophy of your residence hall programming leans heavily toward educational roles, it is unlikely that the total score on this form will adequately reflect the expectations you have for the hall director. This could also reflect, however, differences between your expectations of what the residence hall director's job should be and the reality of what tasks must be done on the job and how frequently.

The appraisal process can err in more subtle ways than omitting important job activities or including irrelevant job activities. Another content validity error is assessing certain qualities of performance inappropriately or in the wrong proportion. A campus activities director may always have her reports and budget requests in on time, but she usually submits an addendum to her report two weeks later, and her budget request always needs drastic revision a month after submission. A performance rating that says she hands in reports and budgets on time would be accurate, but, if no rating is given to the accuracy of reports and budgets, then the rating system does not accurately reflect what her supervisors expect—accurate as well as timely reports. Content validity indicates the congruency between expected job activities, actual job activities, and job behaviors that are assessed in the appraisal process.

Content validity is determined by comparing how well the appraisal process, particularly the assessment tools, match the expected job performance activities. A team of experts, staff, or others can scrutinize the rating form or assessment process to determine whether or not each adequately reflects what is expected of the job and done on the job. To do this, the team should have access to the results of a job analysis or, as a minimum, the job description. The job description should serve as the initial guide in developing a list of what job behaviors need to be observed or rated. It may be inefficient to have a scale or process that looks at all job behaviors; usually what you seek is a representative sample of behavior.

The ability of an assessment tool or process to predict future job performance, called predictive validity, is of interest if the tool and process are being used to make hiring or promotion decisions or to assign staff to specific job positions. You may ask: Does performing well as a residence hall director predict how well the staff member will do as director of residential education? Perhaps the residential education position calls for different skills (such as writing, planning, or conducting workshops) not necessarily a part of a hall director's activities. Does past performance as an adviser to Greek organizations predict how well the person will perform as a campus activities coordinator? Maybe the skills in these two roles overlap sufficiently for good performance with Greek organizations to be a good predictor. Does answering questions about simulated problems in the residence hall predict how the candidate will perform on the job as a residence hall director? Is it possible for a person to be reasonably proficient in responding to simulated problems but not to similar problems in real life—or, on the other hand, to be much more effective in real situations but not outstanding in response to simulations?

In these illustrations, you are more interested in predicting how well the staff member will perform in the future than in making an evaluative judgment about his or her past performance. Predictive validity is an important criterion for selecting a tool or process to help make these decisions. But more sophisticated design and statistical procedures are needed to determine whether or not the tool or process has predictive validity than whether or not it has content validity. You ask yourself, "Does the process (interviews, observations, questionnaires) I am using help me select the right person for the staff positions or the right staff person to promote?" To answer this question, you need a backlog of persons (approximately thirty as a minimum) who have gone through the process so that you can correlate their ratings and scores on the selection instruments to their ratings as staff members. Ideally, those who are ranked higher on the initial selection instruments should also rank higher in job performance. Unfortunately, because you probably used the initial scores as indicators in your initial decision, you will have a limited range of scores to look at among the persons on the job. (In other words, you didn't hire those ranked near the bottom on the initial selection instruments.) This will make it more difficult for the instruments to predict later job performance. Even large companies who hire thirty persons a month find it difficult to determine predictive validity because they do not want to hire everyone without some initial screening.

A truly ideal procedure for determining predictive validity for instruments and procedures—say, those used for hiring student assistants for the residence halls—would involve collecting your interview and questionnaire data on thirty or more students and hiring them all. These data would be filed somewhere so that they would be unavailable to any supervisors or administrators. After you have collected job performance ratings on the student assistants, you would see how each selection measure or process correlated with their job performance. These would be your indices of predictive validity.

Determining content validity is necessary and not difficult. Determining predictive validity is more complex. If you have the opportunity to plan for the long term, then consider trying to collect predictive validity information. The realities of time limitations and other constraints, however, limit what is practically possible.

Reliability. Reliability is the next most important criterion for performance appraisal procedures. Ratings are considered reliable when they remain stable from one rating period to another or from one rater to another rater. Would your ratings of a staff member today be the same as they were last week or as they would be next week? Are the ratings you give a staff member the same as those given by another administrator? Changes in ratings over a period of time can occur for two reasons: because of changes in you, the rater, and in how you interpret the questions or because of changes in the staff member that affect your perceptions of the staff member and, in turn, your rating.

Two administrators may rate a staff member differently because each reads the instructions differently, sees a different side of the staff member's performance, has a different level of knowledge about the staff member, or values different aspects of the staff member's performance. Each administrator's ratings may be affected by other sources of error (such as recency or halo effects). Ratings by supervisors versus those by peers might be expected to differ because they are looking at different aspects of job performance. Poorly constructed rating forms with vague descriptions and unclear instructions, for example, may be read differently by you at different times and can cause two different raters to rate a staff member differently. One rater may think, for example, that "others" in "getting along with others" refers to staff members; another rater may think that it refers to students.

Determining a numerical index of reliability involves correlating ratings of staff members from one time period to another or from one rater to another. It is also possible to look at percentages of agreement among several raters. The more behavioral the rating process is, the greater the reliability will be. Ratings on the question of "How often is the staff member late with written reports?," with response categories of "always" to "never," for example, will be much more reliable than rating responses to an open-ended question, such as "How dependable is the staff member?" Even the "always" to "never" response formats can be made more precise by specifying specific time periods in between (such as once a week, twice a week, once a month, or every other month).

How well the appraisal process sorts staff into a clearly differentiated order is an index of its ability to discriminate. If you wish to use the appraisal information to determine percentages of merit pay or to select the one person to promote, then you want the process to be reasonably reliable. You may wish to look at the ability of the entire appraisal system to indicate to you who is the best staff member or who is the highest ranked, or you may wish to look at how staff rank on specific performance domains (such as budget management or supervising other staff). Is it possible to rank staff members easily overall or on specific aspects of their job performance? The importance of the ability to discriminate depends on the purpose and uses of your assessment process. If your emphasis is on using it for merit salary increases, then you probably want a process that at least clearly separates the super performers from the rest of the pack. If almost all staff members receive superlative ratings, that suggests you have an excellent staff, but it makes it difficult if you have to award pay raises to only the top 10 percent. This dilemma illustrates clearly how the performance appraisal system interacts with other unit policies and in turn how these policies affect the kinds of information needed from the appraisal system. If it is difficult to sort out a top 10 percent of staff members whose performance is clearly significantly higher than the rest, then perhaps the merit pay system needs reexamination.

If you wish to determine who needs special supervision or training, you will want a system that distinguishes the poor performers from the rest. If you want to provide feedback to staff on specific aspects of their performance, then you may not be concerned about their relative rank but may be interested in the reliability of ratings on those particular job aspects.

This brief checklist for evaluating your appraisal system summarizes the concerns addressed in this chapter.

Checklist for Evaluating a Performance Appraisal System

1. Are behavioral job descriptions available for all positions?
2. Are middle-management staff trained in appraisal skills?
3. Is the system behaviorally anchored and job related rather than focusing on personality traits?
4. Is the staff development component separate from compensation decisions?
5. Is the system an ongoing process, not an annual end-of-the-year event?
6. Do middle-management staff:
   a. Spend time defining realistic goals for staff members?
   b. Expect high performance from themselves and others?
   c. Tie individual staff member goals to the unit's goals?
7. Are middle-management staff rewarded for conducting effective performance appraisals?
8. Are the appraisal procedures clear and not too time consuming?
9. Are action plans developed by staff for goal attainment?
10. Are interim interviews held with staff to check progress?
11. Do you have evidence that your appraisal tools and procedures are accurate and reliable?

Conclusion

You don't expect a new staff member to perform perfectly or to fulfill all your expectations during his or her first year. Do not expect more of a performance appraisal system. It is not going to be perfect the first year, nor is it ever going to solve all your personnel problems. Be realistic. A good performance appraisal system is going to take time and energy to develop, maintain, and keep vital. At times it may seem to be more hassle than it is worth. Despite all your efforts, there will be criticisms. Be attentive and responsive to these concerns, but do not despair. Instead, look on the process as a learning tool for you and your staff (Fletcher and Williams, 1985). The bottom line in performance appraisal is whether or not it results in better services and programs for students. If designed and implemented appropriately, your performance appraisal system will improve staff morale, help your staff be more productive, and promote staff professional development. That seems worth the effort.

102

References

Civil Service Commission, Equal Employment Opportunity Commission, Department of Justice, and Department of Labor. "Uniform Guidelines on Employee Selection Procedures." *Federal Register*, 1977, *42*, 65542–65552.

Fletcher, C., and Williams, R. *Performance Appraisal and Career Development.* London: Hutchinson, 1985.

Olson, R. F. *Performance Appraisal.* New York: Wiley, 1981.

Stufflebeam, D. L., and Brethower, D. M. "Improving Personnel Evaluations Through Professional Standards." *Journal of Personnel Evaluation in Education,* 1987, *1* (2), 125–156.

Certain themes run throughout this sourcebook and provide benchmarks for your appraisal system.

Summary Thoughts and Helpful Sources

This sourcebook has not presented *one* model for you to use for performance appraisal, and therefore no acronym has been proposed for representing the main themes. Nevertheless, there are persistent and important themes throughout the volume, and they might well be summarized with the acronym TIPS: *T*raining, *I*nvolvement, *P*rocess, and *S*ystem.

Training

Training management and staff in the process of conducting performance appraisals and of being appraised is essential for an effective performance appraisal system. Since most professionals have had no courses and have had only limited experience in performance appraisal, most of their learning is going to have to come from on-the-job experiences. Most are also going to find the experience an uncomfortable one whether they are the middle manager doing the appraising or the staff member being appraised. This means there is a dire need for workshops and ongoing training programs for student affairs staff to learn about and practice performance appraisal.

R. D. Brown. *Performance Appraisal as a Tool for Staff Development.*
New Directions for Student Services, no. 43. San Francisco: Jossey-Bass, Fall 1988.

Involvement

Because everyone is being appraised and/or is appraising another's performance, it is essential that everyone be involved in the design and implementation of the performance appraisal system. The level of involvement may vary in degree, but, because credibility and usefulness are important ingredients in the acceptance of a performance appraisal system, everyone at least should understand the criteria being used to appraise them, and ideally they should have a say in what those criteria are. Staff may not be experts in instrument design or organizational theory, but they do know much about the constraints and the facilitating conditions that operate in their workplace and influence their work performance.

Process

Too many people see performance appraisal as an event or as a form; it is either the end-of-the-year annual review interview or a form that asks for ratings of someone's performance. Performance appraisal needs to be viewed as an ongoing process. It involves setting goals, providing resources, checking progress, making revisions in goals, and going through the entire cycle again. This process needs to be part of the expectations that middle managers have for themselves; it is something they are responsible for throughout the year, not just at the beginning or primarily at the end of the year. Staff should expect and perhaps even demand appraisal feedback during the year. Appraisal activities designed to foster staff development must be a constant activity if performance appraisal is going to approach fulfilling its promise for improving staff performance and fostering their professional development.

System

Performance appraisal must be viewed as a system as well as a process. As a system, it is a highly interactive set of connected parts. The goals of the unit affect expectations for the staff members of that unit. How those expectations are characterized affects what staff members will do during the year. How much feedback and support the staff get during the year influences how well they perform and what their attitudes are likely to be toward their job and toward their unit's goals. A mishandling of the merit system or a wrong word during an interview can unravel the accomplishments of an entire year's work. Some parts of the system may be more important than others, but each part is essential to an effective performance appraisal system.

Effective performance appraisal takes time and requires a commitment. For many administrators, it is an added-on responsibility. Until it is seen as integral part of their jobs, it will remain something done hurriedly and grudgingly. When performance appraisal is recognized as a critical concern, when administrators see that appropriate training and involvement occur, and when they view performance appraisal as a process and a system, administrators will have significantly enhanced the possibilities that their staff will be vigorous, enthusiastic, and improving professionals.

Sources

Performance appraisal goes back to when Adam made a comment about the relative accomplishments of Cain and Abel, but published resources do not go back quite as far. As might be expected, most of the publications focus on business and industrial settings. In education, the emphasis is on faculty or teacher evaluation. The most relevant sources of those available are selected publications in the business setting. Despite the availability of sources related to the business world, these sources do not offer magic formulas or grand solutions. A few are highly sophisticated in their analysis but not necessarily surprising in their conclusions. The sources listed represent a broad spectrum, including a few that are primarily of the how-to-do-it variety, some that review previous literature, and a few that examine the theoretical and philosophical issues related to performance appraisal.

Baird, L. S., Beatty, R. W., and Schneier, C. E. (eds.). *The Performance Appraisal Sourcebook*. Amherst, Mass.: Human Resources Development Press, 1982.
    This book contains reprinted articles on major issues in performance appraisal and excellent case studies and role-playing situations that can be used for training workshops and discussions. It is probably the best single how-to source available.

Berk, R. A. (ed.). *Performance Assessment*. Baltimore, Md.: Johns Hopkins University Press, 1986.
    This is not a how-to book, but it does contain a thoughtful and provocative examination of the major issues in performance appraisal.

DeVries, D. L., Morrison, A. M., Shullman, S. L., and Gerlach, M. L. *Performance Appraisal on the Line*. New York: Wiley, 1981.
    This is a well-documented, comprehensive look at appraisal and includes a history of performance appraisal.

Kirkpatrick, D. L. *How to Improve Performance Through Appraisal and Coaching*. New York: AMACOM, 1982.

The author discusses performance appraisal from a coaching perspective. The book has numerous helpful checklists, sample forms, and case studies.

Latham, G. P., and Wexley, K. E. *Increasing Productivity Through Performance Appraisal*. Reading, Mass.: Addison-Wesley, 1981.

These authors provide comprehensive coverage of the appraisal process from instrumentation design through interviewing. This book is somewhat more theoretical than other sources, and the authors support their suggestions with research data; they also carefully address legal considerations throughout the book.

Lazer, R. I., and Wikstrom, W. S. *Appraising Managerial Performance: Current Practices and Future Directions*. New York: Conference Board, 1977.

Although perhaps a bit dated, this source presents a comprehensive picture of appraisal practices in the business community based on an extensive survey.

Olson, R. F. *Performance Appraisal: A Guide to Greater Productivity*. New York: Wiley, 1981.

This book focuses on appraisal as a means of improving staff performance and offers helpful sections on the interview process. The author stresses the importance of clear communications and staff involvement.

Sashkin, M. *Assessing Performance Appraisal*. San Diego, Calif.: University Associates, 1981.

This is an excellent source on the development of assessment instruments and includes discussions of sources of error and how to reduce error. It also offers a comprehensive annotated bibliography.

Index